Gender and Genre in
GERTRUDE STEIN

——Gender and Genre in——
GERTRUDE STEIN

Franziska Gygax

Contributions in Women's Studies, number 169

Greenwood Press
Westport, Connecticut • London

Library of Congress Cataloging-in-Publication Data

Gygax, Franziska.
    Gender and genre in Gertrude Stein / Franziska Gygax.
       p. cm.—(Contributions in women's studies, ISSN 0147–104X ;
  no. 169)
    Includes bibliographical references and index.
    ISBN 0–313–30755–5 (alk. paper)
    1. Stein, Gertrude, 1874–1946—Criticism and interpretation.
  2. Women and literature—United States—History—20th century.
  3. Gender identity in literature. 4. Literary form. I. Title.
  II. Series.
  PS3537.T323Z63   1998
  818'.5209—dc21   98–12150

British Library Cataloguing in Publication Data is available.

Library of Congress Catalog Card Number: 98–12150
ISBN: 0–313–30755–5
ISSN: 0147–104X

First published in 1998

Greenwood Press, 88 Post Road West, Westport, CT 06881
An imprint of Greenwood Publishing Group, Inc.

Printed in the United States of America

The paper used in this book complies with the
Permanent Paper Standard issued by the National
Information Standards Organization (Z39.48–1984).

10 9 8 7 6 5 4 3 2

Copyright Acknowledgments

The author and the publisher gratefully acknowledge permission for use of the following material:

From *Everybody's Autobiography* by Gertrude Stein. Copyright 1937 and renewed 1965 by Alice B. Toklas. Reprinted by permission of Random House, Inc.

Excerpts from Gertrude Stein's *The Making of Americans, Stanzas in Meditation,* and *Everybody's Autobiography* reprinted with permission from the Law Offices of Levin & Gann on behalf of the Estate of Gertrude Stein.

Excerpts from *Women in Search for Literary Space,* edited by Gudrun Grabher and Maureen Devine, 1992, reprinted by permission of Gunter Narr Verlag.

Contents

Acknowledgments

I owe many thanks to many different people who helped me at different stages of this project. My special thanks go to Catharine R. Stimpson for her illuminating and creative advice on how to work with Stein. I am also grateful to Hartwig Isernhagen and Peter Halter for their critical readings of my manuscript and their helpful suggestions. Hans Jürg Kupper's critical comments on each chapter provided invaluable suggestions. I thank Anne Blonstein for her thorough and painstaking reading that greatly improved the manuscript. Sabine Cassani and Anne Zimmermann read parts of the draft; I am grateful for their critical comments and their unstinting support. Harriet Chessman and Marianne DeKoven, two Stein critics from whom I also learnt a lot, received me warmly during my stay at Princeton in 1990–1991.

A three-year fellowship from the Swiss Foundation for the Sciences and the Humanities enabled me to spend eighteen months at Princeton University. I also owe thanks to the Uarda Frutiger Foundation of the "Freiwillige Akademische Gesellschaft," Basel, and the Max Geldner Foundation, Basel, for their generous financial support, and to the Cooper Foundation, Basel, for a contribution toward the publication of this book.

I am grateful to Willi Matter who carefully and meticulously prepared the final manuscript. I have been fortunate with Jamie Nan Thaman as copy editor, with Linda Ellis as production editor, and with Marcia Goldstein from Greenwood Press; I express my gratitude to them.

For permission to quote from Gertrude Stein's notebooks I am grateful to the Estate of Gertrude Stein and to the Yale Collection of American Literature, Beinecke Library, Yale University.

Finally, I would like to thank Michael Müller for his supportive and creative companionship with Stein; our two sons, Jonas and Julian, also contributed to this book: Jonas as a respondent to Stein's *The World Is Round*, and Julian as an "excreative" producer of sounds and words when language became his mediator.

Abbreviations

Introduction:
Gendered Genre

Gertrude Stein's works comprise many different genres and most do not have clearly defined traits of a specific genre according to classic genre theory. Stein herself explicitly calls many of her works "plays," "operas," or "novels"; thus, it seems that she intended her works to be read with certain generic[1] expectations in mind, be it only to have them undermined. Indeed, most of the expectations related to a specific genre are never met in her works; on the contrary, in some of her plays and operas, not even the most conspicuous rule, namely that a play have a character, is obeyed. Of course, breaking the laws of a genre is not unusual—generic transgressions have always appeared in literary texts. Indeed, "every text is a member of one or more genres,"[2] and in postmodern writings the blurring and transgression of genres are primary characteristics. But Stein's generic transgressions call for particular attention because they are very radical and because they can be related to gender-specific traits of Stein's writing. Many of her more hermetic and associative works can only be read when gender as a theoretical category is used. As it is especially difficult to subsume these texts under a particular genre, and because Stein raises questions about gender hierarchies, I will suggest a direct relation between gender and genre. Hierarchies, classifications, and categories are fundamental characteristics of both gender and genre. In this book I want to explore the reasons why Stein was inevitably confronted with questions about both generic and gender categories.

The notion of gender "is far, however, from reaching a state of consensus," as Elaine Showalter already cautioned in 1989.[3] The recent Butler debate,[4] which was triggered by Judith Butler's statement that gender is always performative and intentional and is an act that is produced by the reiteration and reproduction of cultural norms,[5] illustrates that gender is indeed an ongoing process and not a fixed category. There is definitely no end of gender as a critical category of analysis as some feminist theorists feared after Butler's provocative but also rewarding critique of the sex-gender system. The concept of the sociocultural construction is criticized because it is actually based on the assumption that there is something before the construction, namely "the body" or "sexuality," but even our notions of the body are socially and culturally determined.

The notion of gender as performance is crucial to lesbianism as it opens up the category "lesbian" and undermines confining definitions. For Stein as a lesbian writer, this notion of performance, of acting in/by language, can be made useful for her writing because her texts constantly explore problems of identity that are intricately related to performance. "Sexual difference," which is often used together with gender, is concerned with questions about differences in language, identity, and subject and relies on theories developed by Jacques Lacan and, from a more feminist point of view, Julia Kristeva. I shall especially rely on Kristeva's concept of the pre-Oedipal as the presymbolic that can disrupt symbolic, that is, patriarchal discourse.[6] The ever-returning question of how to theorize sexual difference, especially within homosexuality, also remains a crucial issue in "Queer Studies," and Stein's constant questioning of identity categories reminds us of the problematic implications when we use a specific term and thereby claim representativeness and/or exclusion.[7]

Western genre[8] theory illustrates that a genre is always embedded historically and, what is often forgotten, politically: "Like any other institution, genres bring to light the constitutive features of the society to which they belong."[9] There-fore, it is not surprising that many women writers used genres that were appropriate to their social and cultural position. Virginia Woolf's famous state-ment about the nineteenth-century woman novelist is a case in point:

Fiction was, as fiction still is, the easiest thing for a woman to write. Nor is it difficult to find the reason. A novel is the least concentrated form of art. A novel can be taken up or put down more easily than a play or a poem. George Eliot left her work to nurse her father. Charlotte Brontë put down her pen to pick the eyes out of the potatoes. And living as she did in the common sitting-room, surrounded by people, a woman was trained to use her mind in observation and upon the analysis of character. She was trained to be a novelist and not to be a poet.[10]

With regard to such observations, Celeste Schenck aptly speaks of a politics of genre[11] and proposes that feminist genre theory should question the criteria of form and norm used for the labelling of genres. She describes the (gendered) implications of traditional genre theory:

[B]eneath the Western will to taxonomize lies not only a defensive history of exclusions that constitute a political ideology but also a fetishizing of aesthetic purity—not unlike that which this culture maintains of virginity—which has distinctly gendered overtones. Pure genres, like biological genders, had best remain discrete and intact. Mixed, unclas-sifiable, blurred, or hybrid genres, like impure, anomalous, or monstrous genders, have traditionally offered up problems to their diagnosticians.[12]

The relation between gender and genre is also explicitly expressed by Jacques Derrida, who points out that genre always implies "sexual difference between the feminine and masculine genre/gender" and that this implication is still mirrored in the connotation of German and French words such as *Gattung*, *gattieren* ("to mix," "to classify"), *begatten* ("to couple"), and the French *genre*, which always includes gender.[13] Derrida's main concern is to show how genre can never be dealt with as an isolated issue and that, by definition, aspects of difference are raised as soon as a particular text is attributed to a genre. Thus, as participation always implies difference, a genre never remains the same after a text has been attributed to it. Yet, Derrida does not elaborate on how *sexual* difference relates to genre and on the impact gender can have on the formation of a genre. He only postulates an inevitable, though paradoxical, violation of the law of genre ("genres are not to be mixed") because "a principle of contamination, a law of impurity, a parasitical economy" is inherent in "the law of the law of genre."[14] In her essay "Post-Scriptum—High-Modern," Joan Retallack also refers to our limited understanding of the dichotomies of gender and genre and hints at a close relationship between the two, but she does not investigate this issue further.[15]

Feminist critics have commented on the relationship between gender and one particular genre, namely the autobiographical mode of writing. Various studies on the gender implications of women's autobiographies have shown that the genre "autobiography" cannot be theorized without taking into account the sex of the autobiographer.[16] Some critics writing on the theory of female autobiography conclude that there is a close link between the two genres of autobiography and poetry. Emily Dickinson, Sylvia Plath, or Adrienne Rich are mentioned as examples writing the poetic self as subject. Another study dealing with gender and genre is Helen Carr's anthology *From My Guy to Sci-Fi: Genre and Women's Writing in the Postmodern World,* but as the title implies, it focuses on women's writings of the postmodern period only.[17] Furthermore, it is an anthology of essays, each of which deals with a particular genre used by women writers, and thus the relationship of gender and genre is not the main focus. Shari Benstock investigates the gender implications of the epistolary genre and the connection between "letters" and "literature."[18] Linda Kauffman explores how letter writing can be a tool (genre) for women to escape their socially constrained lives and to express their desire(s) that were suppressed by social norms.[19] Although in some of these studies a more general theoretical framework of the relationship between gender and genre is assumed, this relationship needs to be investigated in more detail.

Mary Gerhart's recent book *Genre Choices, Gender Questions* is the first comprehensive study on this theme. Gerhart describes the intersections of gender/genre by applying both a gender and genre analysis to a literary text. But her inquiry does not focus on radical generic deviations, although in her last chapter she deals with examples of the "new novel," that is, writings by John Barth or Joan Didion. Gerhart never questions the issue of genre with regard to a specific text. Nevertheless, her approach, which she calls "genre testing and gender testing,"[20] is highly informative as far as generic and gender conventions are concerned. She is convinced that both gender and genre are "at the center of critical interpretation" and that an analysis of these categories can avoid misinterpretation of a text and at the same time can trigger "maximum reinterpretation."[21] Genre and gender testing is based on a reader's ability to recognize generic conventions and on his/her awareness of gender issues.[22]

The close interaction between gender and genre can be further scrutinized by looking at formally experimental texts by women writers of the modernist period (e.g., Djuna Barnes, H.D., or Gertrude Stein), as such texts often defy straightforward generic categorization. Challenging generic classification often goes hand in hand with a radical position with regard to tradition and the canon. Tradition and canon are mainly shaped by patriarchal law, and therefore, women who write against tradition and search for new forms are most likely to challenge the symbolic realm of language that is characterized by patriarchal structures.[23] Thus, texts undermining generic classifications and definitions may also reveal subversive strategies against phallogocentrism. What is the relation between this doubt toward generic classification and the challenging of phallogocentric rules? Does the "subversive intent" necessarily entail generic transgression?

My theoretical framework is mainly rooted in American feminist thought—above all, in American feminist literary criticism. I shall point out its usefulness for my particular interest in Stein, but I shall not comment on the merits of the various critical positions within this tradition.

Among the modernist women writers, Gertrude Stein is the one who most radically experiments with language. Indeed, many of her experimental texts are so provocative that a "subversive intent" seems to be at the core of her writing. To label Stein a modernist writer is a risky undertaking because so-called modernist criteria do not necessarily apply to all of her texts. The issue of genre is the main reason why Stein cannot simply be placed within the boundaries of modernism.[24] In modernist discourse, the question of genre was always a main concern; modernist texts revitalized the traditional genres, renewing them or adapting them to their own generic ideas.[25] Postmodernism, on the other hand, seems to demonstrate a dissolution of generic boundaries, a reluctance to yield to any kind of generic classification. In this respect, Gertrude Stein, writing in the modernist period, is obviously closer to postmodern writers than to her "peers." What are the reasons for this avant-garde position and in what ways does gender contribute to this singular experiment with language? These are questions that will be addressed in the course of this study.

The feminist critic's assumption that sexual difference is inscribed in writing is linked with the crucial issue of authorship and subjectivity. Therefore, in dealing with a writer like Gertrude Stein, whose lesbian sexuality is part of her identity, one must explore the specific psychosexual structures of her texts in relation to her specific sexuality. Her experiments with language are related to her situation as a lesbian woman writer who positioned herself not outside of patriarchy but inside it, without submitting to its linguistic codes. Instead, she created what one might term "antilanguage."[26] As recent feminist criticism on Stein has shown, this antilanguage can be much better understood when we consider the tensions and contradictions deriving from Stein's marginalized position in culture.

The feminist approaches to the analysis of Stein's antilanguage are as complex and multifarious as the different positions in feminist theory. I want to discuss the most controversial, and crucial, aspect among them, namely the notion that language is phallogocentric.[27] Feminist critics influenced by French-language feminist theoreticians such as Julia Kristeva, Luce Irigaray, or Hélène Cixous believe that the semiotic or pre-symbolic is strongly connected with the "feminine" insofar as the semiotic is associated with the mother's body before the child enters the symbolic order (Kristeva's position). They emphasize the importance and influence of the woman's body from which a text can spring (Irigaray's and Cixous' position). Various feminist critics are worried by essentialist dangers lurking in these theories. In her critical account of French feminist theory, Rita Felski expresses her doubts concerning Kristeva's position:

This argument seems to me unsatisfactory in that it reinscribes at the level of theoretical abstraction those gender specifications whose inevitability feminists should be calling into question; from the social given that young children are primarily cared for by the mother, it extrapolates an abstract dualism grounded in the equation of the masculine with culture and the feminine with the body and the presocial, an extrapolation with strong ideological implications.[28]

This important critique must be heard, but I still believe that Kristeva's theory of the semiotic is extremely useful with regard to many of Stein's textual strategies. However, it is also necessary to focus on the historical, social, and material situation of the female author. Then, the analysis of the (modernist) woman writer's situation[29] can support the hypothesis that her text is open, polysemic, disruptive, and, thus, subversive.

The relationship between a "feminine" text and its subversive and revolutionary practice needs further investigation. The exemplary writers, in whose texts Kristeva detects the disruptive force, are all male. Kristeva herself points out that it is almost impossible for women writers to acquire the same status as these male writers because they are trapped in a double bind: if they decide to subvert the patriarchal rules, they risk losing their subversive energy, that is, the semiotic against the symbolic, because they must yield totally to the paternal identification necessary for access to this very order.[30] Without the paternal identification, they cannot use their voices. Although she recommends not capitulating before this dilemma, she admits that avoidance of it is almost impossible for women in the present situation. It is perhaps not coincidental that Kristeva then proceeds to examine women writers who committed suicide (Virginia Woolf, Marina Tsvetayeva, and Sylvia Plath). Yet, she mentions those women who "have been able to serve or overthrow the socio-historic order by playing at being supermen. A few enjoy it: the most active, the most effective, the 'homosexual' women (whether they know it or not)."[31] With regard to Stein, I cannot but focus on Kristeva's observation about the homosexual woman because Stein's ego was indeed male-identified. Stein seems to have embraced the dilemma that Kristeva discusses, without losing or sacrificing subversive force.

For these reasons, Kristeva's comments on the subversive force of the "feminine" text will still be guidelines for my analysis of Stein's texts, but I shall combine them with a focus on the social and ideological conditions that shaped Stein's writing. That genre plays an essential role in this analysis of textual production should be obvious when we recall the preliminary observations about genre criticism and about the relation between gender and genre. Specific social and ideological conditions can be the reasons why a particular genre is chosen, transformed, or ignored altogether. Similarly, these conditions shape and influence the ways gender is constructed.

Stein's own statements about genre or genre-related issues hint at her uneasiness about generic categories. The texts containing such statements are often very radical expressions of her dissatisfaction with traditional genres or are themselves generic transgressions.

Stein's theoretical statements about writing are deeply rooted in her wish to *explain* her own ideas about literature and writing. But her theoretical essays on writing cannot simply be labelled "essays" because they frequently contain exclusively autobiographical passages. A "blurring of genres"[32] can even be detected in a text that is intended to explain her other texts. In this way, a theoretical text such as *How to Write*, which is highly hermetic, associative, and difficult to understand, alludes to some very personal events or attitudes. An autobiographical text such as *Everybody's Autobiography*, on the other hand, also contains statements about Stein's attitude toward literary genres. Therefore, a distinction between explicitly "theoretical" and more "personal" statements cannot be made; Stein's opinions on genre cannot simply be subsumed under the category "essays." Indeed, this "mixing" of genres is one of the main issues that is raised by postmodern inquiry. As Ralph Cohen points out, even a theoretical article like "Dancing through the Minefield: Some Observations on the Theory, Practice, and Politics of a Feminist Literary Criticism" by Annette Kolodny "can . . . contain autobiographical discourses."[33] This "blurring of genres" goes hand in hand with Celeste Schenck's description of genres as "often-complementary discourses";[34] she points out for example that poetic texts by women writers are equally concerned with subjectivity as women's autobiography. In Kolodny's case the combination of the more personal together with a theoretical procedure challenges the notion of objectivity, as she makes clear in the course of her argument. Feminist criticism, Kolodny claims, questions so-called objective statements in literary criticism.[35] This example illustrates that the "blurring of genres" not only challenges generic expectations but also undermines notions of rules, classifications, or "objective" boundaries. Thus, a typically postmodern text such as the one by Annette Kolodny shares one of its most obvious traits—generic challenge—with a text by Stein written some sixty years earlier.

In *Everybody's Autobiography*, Stein tells us how she told Thornton Wilder while walking through Paris "that what worried [her] was narration."[36] This passage reveals that she no longer believes in the form of the novel and she therefore suggests to young writers "to write essays, after all since characters are of no importance why not just write meditations, meditations are always interesting, neither character nor identity are necessary to him who meditates."[37] This example of generic mistrust toward narrative illustrates Stein's concern with problems of describing persons or dealing with identity. Meditations seem to be attractive to Stein because they are not subject to a fixed chronology of events and seldom describe the development of a character.[38] In her lecture "Portraits and Repetitions," she explains why she began to compose portraits and why she wrote portraits of objects as, for example, in *Tender Buttons*. Such comments on generic doubts or preferences are dispersed throughout Stein's works. They all share deep reservations about conventional, traditional modes of writing because they do not seem adequate to her to *narrate* a story or to *describe* a person or object.

Stein comments on almost every literary genre and most of these comments reveal that hardly any genre could satisfy her needs and goals. Her first, most direct, references to genre can be found in *How to Write*, composed in separate parts between 1927 and 1931, the year of its first publication. In "Regular Regularly in Narrative" (1927), Stein playfully explores the possibilities and limits of narrative. Her comments are neither straightforward nor obviously deductive, yet she gradually comes to the conclusion that narrative does not satisfy her because "narratives are continuous"[39] and she implicitly denies that something can be depicted in a continuous way. The artificiality of a concept such as continuity is the reason for Stein's dissatisfaction with the form of narrative:

A narrative might be what if older older than they were said said so might be said so might be said so. A narrative is as they wish. A great many people to see Africa. To see Africa. Glenway Westcott to see Africa. A narrative of to see Africa a narrative of to see to see Africa. What is their difference. (*HTW*, p. 269)

This example illustrates Stein's emphasis on the inherent discontinuity of a narrative: If we want to tell something we can never rely on *one* narrative line; a story on Westcott's[40] trip to Africa also entails a story of "seeing Africa" and this again makes comments on "seeing" necessary ("to see to see"), and so on. To present a narrative line would require relying on a chronological order that is always a superimposed order and selective as well.

A more radical statement about the illusion of linearity can be found in *The Geographical History of America*: "There is no reason why chapters should succeed each other since nothing succeeds another, not now any more. In the old novels yes but not now any more."[41] Stein's insistence that there is no successive order is largely based on her concept of time. Time is not conceived as something that can be partitioned into past, present, and future. Indeed, Stein's rupture of any temporal structure is similar to the notion of time in French feminism as most explicitly expressed by Kristeva: Since "[t]he symbolic order—the order of verbal communication, the paternal order of genealogy—is a temporal order,"[42] women who try to disrupt this order speak "beyond present-past-future."[43] The similarity between Stein's rupture and subversion of temporal linearity and Kristeva's statement about paternal time is striking, although Kristeva never mentions Gertrude Stein when writing about avant-garde women writers.[44] Both Stein and Kristeva suggest that disrupting time also means disrupting language. Stein's distrust of temporal linearity is always closely connected with her wish to tell us "what happened"[45] without having to rely on a narrative line; thus, she is bound to "break the sequence" *and* "the sentence."[46] Dismissing chronology and linearity implies a dismissal of the traditional genres because they all rely on hierarchies and taxonomies, that is, an ordering principle.

Stein's challenging approach to genre is also very creative: Apart from using almost all existing literary labels including a detective story and a children's book, she invents new genres and names them: the portrait and the landscape.[47] It is probably not a coincidence that two other influential women writers of her time also composed portraits: H.D. and Djuna Barnes.[48] In the chapters dealing with Stein's portraits I shall argue that her portrait writing reflects an attempt at describing "real" persons as they are "inside." To find out "inside every one what was in them" (*LA*, p. 183), Stein relied on her capability of talking *and* listening. Talking and listening are not only capabilities that Stein considered to be the "essence of genius" (*LA*, p. 170) but are also necessary requisites for communication, for dialogue. As Harriet Chessman emphasizes in her book *The Public Is Invited to Dance: Representation, the Body, and Dialogue in Gertrude Stein*, dialogue is a main characteristic in Stein's works. Dialogue can take various forms and functions, but it always creates a connection between somebody or something and somebody or something else.[49] This "connecting" dialogue, which creates intimacy, shares similarities with the presymbolic where the child is closely "connected" with its mother. Stein's portrait writing is one example of her dialogic approach to writing, opposed to the monologic dominance characteristic of phallogocentrism.

In the following chapters I shall explore the various genres Stein used. Trying to enumerate these genres confronts one with the problem of genre definition. I have decided to choose one or two more or less representative texts that have an explicit generic name and follow Stein's generic labelling as she herself intentionally (and playfully) titles her writings according to genres: *Ida A Novel*, *A Circular Play*, *Four Saints in Three Acts*, *Everybody's Autobiography*, *The Geographical History of America*, *Blood on the Dining-Room Floor* (which she calls a "detective story" in "Why I Like Detective Stories").[50] Using these classifications enables me to elucidate Stein's generic subversions and to comment on her "re-creation"[51] of genre and gender. Her playful and radical exploration of both categories challenges attempts at rigid definitions. I will argue that her deconstructive approach to genre is always related to the way(s) gender is inscribed in her texts.

The first Part looks at an early and a late novel; in Chapter 1 on *The Making of Americans*, I will demonstrate that Stein does not follow a patrilinear narrative line and that the family whose history she wants to tell literally falls apart.

My theoretical framework for this analysis is based on the feminist debate about the female writing subject and its relation to its text. My discussion in Chapter 2 of *Ida A Novel* focuses on the ways identity is constructed through the notion of twins. I shall try to describe how the character of Ida and *Ida* the book merge; not surprisingly, the question about genre becomes crucial.

In Part 2 I want to explore Stein's so-called dramatic works and investigate how her concern to create immediacy in language is related to a postmodern approach to plays. Her two early plays, *A Circular Play* and *Ladies' Voices*, and her late opera, *The Mother of Us All*, serve as examples of Stein's radical transformation of the genre "play," or "opera." For my analysis of the two early plays the notion of the lesbian subject will be employed in order to focus on the gender of the many unidentified speakers (or characters) involved. Stein's lesbianism as it pervades her writing calls for this theoretical framework, and it is especially visible/audible in these short plays as Stein frequently uses her private (lesbian) vocabulary for female lovemaking.

Part 3 is devoted to Stein's autobiographies and biography. I want to show how Stein's (re)presentation of the self is intricately intertwined with many other "selves," above all with the one of her companion Alice B. Toklas. Furthermore, the question of literary creativity with regard to this intermingling of selves will be addressed.

In Part 4, which deals with the detective story *Blood on the Dining-Room Floor* and the poetic work *Stanzas in Meditation*, I want to demonstrate how and why the issue of genre becomes so problematic for Stein's writing. I shall rely on the notion of difference and *différance* in order to discuss Stein's use of difference, the dominating topic of *Stanzas in Meditation*.

Part 6, which follows the conclusion, looks at Stein's children's book *The World Is Round*. The reasons for this unusual sequence will be elucidated through the very discussion of this book that is concerned with roundness and circularity.

My different reading(s) of gender and genre should provide insight into Stein's creation of different writing(s).

NOTES

1. Mary Gerhart uses the adjective "genric" in order "to emphasize the functions of the concept of genre interpretation. The conventional form *generic* has come to connote aspects such as nonspecificity and common variety, aspects unrelated to the process of interpretation" (Gerhart, *Genre Choices, Gender Questions* [Norman: University of Oklahoma Press, 1992], p. 228, no. 8). As I believe that the genre question cannot be approached without considering issues of interpretation, I will not make such a distinction and thus will only use *generic* throughout my study.

2. Ralph Cohen, "Do Postmodern Genres Exist?" in *Postmodern Genres*, ed. Marjorie Perloff (Norman: University of Oklahoma Press, 1989), p. 14.

3. Elaine Showalter, introduction to her anthology *Speaking of Gender* (New York: 1989), p. 3.

4. See, for example, *Feminist Contentions: A Philosophical Exchange*, ed. Seyla Benhabib et al. (New York: Routledge, 1995).

5. Judith Butler, *Gender Trouble: Feminism and the Subversion of Identity* (New York: Routledge, 1990), pp. 24–25; and *Bodies That Matter: On the Discursive Limits of "Sex"* (New York: Routledge, 1993), p. 2.

6. For the notion of sexual difference, see my Chapter 12 on *Stanzas in Meditation* with its topic "difference."

7. For a critical discussion of the term "lesbian," in which it is described as outside of "woman" and "man," see Cheshire Calhoun's essay "The Gender Closet: The Lesbian Disappearance under the Sign 'Women,'" in *Lesbian Subjects*, ed. Martha Vicinus (Bloomington: Indiana University Press, 1996), pp. 209–32.

8. For an informative and comprehensive study on the theory of genre, see Alastar Fowler, *Kinds of Literature: An Introduction to the Theory of Genres and Modes* (Oxford: Oxford University Press, 1982). The following studies also provide a survey of the history of genre: Heather Dubrow, *Genre* (London: Methuen, 1982); Adena Rosmarin, *The Power of Genre* (Minneapolis: University of Minnesota Press, 1985); Cesare Segre, with the collaboration of Tomaso Kemeny, *Introduction to the Analysis of the Literary Text*, trans. John Meddemmen (Bloomington: Indiana University Press, 1988); or Todorov's *Genres in Discourse*, trans. Catherine Porter (Cambridge: Cambridge University Press, 1990); Mary Gerhart's recent study, *Genre Choices, Gender Questions* (Norman: University of Oklahoma Press, 1992), also provides a very concise introduction to the theory of genre; see Chapter 2.

9. Todorov, *Genres in Discourse*, p. 19.

10. Virginia Woolf, *Women and Writing*, ed. Michèlle Barrett (New York: Harcourt Brace Jovanovich, 1979), p. 46.

11. Celeste Schenck, "All of a Piece: Women's Poetry and Autobiography," in *Life/Lines: Theorizing Women's Autobiography*, ed. Bella Brodzki and Celeste Schenck (Ithaca, NY: Cornell University Press, 1988), p. 282.

12. Ibid., pp. 283–84.

13. Jacques Derrida, "The Law of Genre," *Critical Inquiry* 7, no. 1 (Autumn 1980): 74.

14. Ibid., 55, 59.

15. Joan Retallack, "Post-Scriptum–High-Modern," in *Postmodern Genres*, ed. Marjorie Perloff (Norman: University of Oklahoma Press, 1989) p. 271. Retallack also mentions the fact that "Derrida engages in a fascinating discussion of relationships between gender and genre" in his essay "The Law of Genre," (p. 273).

16. I mention only three recent influential studies in this field at this point because I will deal with women's autobiographies in more detail when discussing Stein's *The Autobiography of Alice B. Toklas*. The three are: *The Private Self: Theory and Practice of Women's Autobiographical Writings*, ed. Shari Benstock (Chapel Hill: University of North Carolina Press, 1988); *Life/Lines: Theorizing Women's Autobiography*, ed. Bella Brodzki and Celeste Schenck; and Sidonie Smith, *A Poetics of Women's Autobiography: Marginality and the Fictions of Self-Representations* (Bloomington: Indiana University Press, 1987).

17. *From My Guy to Sci-Fi: Genre and Women's Writing in the Postmodern World*, ed. Helen Carr (London: Pandora, 1989).

18. Shari Benstock, "From Letters to Literature: La Carte Postale in the Epistolary Genre," *Genre* 18, no. 3 (Fall 1985): 257–95.

19. Linda Kauffman, *Discourses of Desire: Gender, Genre, and Epistolary Fictions* (Ithaca, NY: Cornell University Press, 1986).

20. Mary Gerhart, *Genre Choices*, especially chapter 7, pp. 186–222.

21. Ibid., p. 7.

22. Gerhart refers to gendered readers who must have certain kinds of competence, e.g., they are aware of a narrator's gendered perspective, or they reflect the role women play in a text. Furthermore, they must be alert to the way language is used by men and women. See Gerhart, p. 163.

23. Although I attribute subversive force to the texts of these writers, I want to emphasize that not all experimental texts are inherently feminine or feminist. See also the discussions of this issue in Rita Felski, *Beyond Feminist Aesthetics: Feminist Literature and Social Change* (Cambridge, MA: Harvard University Press, 1989), pp. 3–7; or Shari Benstock, *Textualizing the Feminine: On the Limits of Genre* (Norman: University of Oklahoma Press, 1991), pp. xxix–xxx.

24. See also Shari Benstock's comment on the difficulties of placing Stein within the movement of modernism in "Beyond the Reaches of Feminist Criticism: A Letter from Paris," in *Feminist Issues in Literary Scholarship*, ed. Shari Benstock (Bloomington: Indiana University Press, 1987), pp. 25–27.

25. Compare Marjorie Perloff, *Postmodern Genres*, p. 3.

26. Benstock, *Textualizing the Feminine*, p. xxiv, and Catharine R. Stimpson, "The Somagrams of Gertrude Stein," in *Critical Essays on Gertrude Stein*, ed. Michael J. Hoffman (Boston: G. K. Hall, 1986), p. 191. Stimpson uses M.A.K. Halliday's term "anti-language."

27. Using this term I rely on Luce Irigaray for whom "that phallogocentric mode of signifying the female sex perpetually reproduces phantasms of its own self-amplifying desire. Instead of a self-limiting linguistic gesture that grants alterity or difference to women, phallogocentrism offers a name to eclipse the feminine and take its place" (Judith Butler, *Gender Trouble: Feminism and the Subversion of Identity* [New York: Routledge, 1990], pp. 12–13).

28. Rita Felski, *Beyond Feminist Aesthetics*, p. 35.

29. Susan Suleiman also emphasizes this point in her account of writers of the avant-garde. See *Subversive Intent: Gender, Politics, and the Avant-Garde* (Cambridge, MA: Harvard University Press, 1990), p. 18.

30. See Julia Kristeva, "About Chinese Women" [1974], in *The Kristeva Reader*, ed. Toril Moi (New York: Columbia University Press, 1986), p. 155.

31. Ibid.

32. Clifford Geertz, "Blurred Genres: The Refiguration of Social Thought," *The American Scholar* 49 (Spring 1980): 165.

33. Ralph Cohen, "Do Postmodern Genres Exist?" *Postmodern Genres*, ed. Marjorie Perloff, p. 15.

34. Celeste Schenck, "All of a Piece," in *Life/Lines*, p. 286.

35. Ralph Cohen, "Do Postmodern Genres Exist?" *Postmodern Genres*, ed. Marjorie Perloff, p. 15.

36. Gertrude Stein, *Everybody's Autobiography* (New York: Random House, 1937), p. 107.

37. Ibid., p. 102.

38. In the chapter dealing with Stein's work *Stanzas in Meditation*, I provide a broad definition of the term.

39. Gertrude Stein, *How to Write* (New York: Dover Publications, 1975), p. 269. All subsequent references will be cited in the text.

40. Glenway Westcott is one of the young writers mentioned in *The Autobiography of Alice B. Toklas* (New York: Random House, 1961), pp. 200, 219. It is not clear whether

Westcott actually went to Africa or whether this was just made up by Stein in order to give an example.

41. Gertrude Stein, *The Geographical History of America* (New York: Random House, 1936), p. 54. All subsequent references will be cited in the text.

42. Julia Kristeva, "About Chinese Women" [1974], in *The Kristeva Reader*, ed. Toril Moi, p. 152.

43. Ibid., p. 155. Kristeva continues to emphasize the double bind women have to cope with: If women attempt to refuse the role as the unconscious "truth" of patriarchy, then they are already entrapped in the symbolic order, that is, they identify with the Father and support this very order.

44. See also Dinnah Pladott's remark on the same issue. Dinnah Pladott, "Gertrude Stein: Exile, Feminism, Avant-Garde in the American Theater," in *Modern American Drama: The Female Canon*, ed. June Schlueter (Rutherford, NJ: Fairleigh Dickinson University Press, 1990), p. 11.

45. Gertrude Stein, *Lectures in America* (Boston: Beacon Press, 1985), p. 121. All subsequent references will be cited in the text, preceded by *LA*, and refer to this edition.

46. Writing about Mary Carmichael in *A Room of One's Own* (London: The Hogarth Press, 1954), Virginia Woolf states: "First she broke the sentence; now she has broken the sequence" (p. 122). Rachel Blau DuPlessis also uses these expressions for the title of one of her chapters in *Writing beyond the Ending: Narrative Strategies of Twentieth-Century Women Writers* (Bloomington: Indiana University Press, 1985).

47. In Part 2 on plays I comment on Stein's use of the term.

48. See also Gisela Ecker's comment in "Gertrude Stein, Hilda Doolittle (H.D.) und Djuna Barnes: Drei Amerikanerinnen in Europa," in *Weiblichkeit und Avantgarde*, ed. Inge Stephan and Sigrid Weigel (Hamburg: Argument-Verlag, 1987), p. 52.

49. Harriet S. Chessman, *The Public Is Invited to Dance: Representation, the Body, and Dialogue in Gertrude Stein* (Stanford, CA: Stanford University Press, 1989), pp. 1–3. I suggest that this relationship between inside and outside can also be seen in the light of private or public as Gilles Deleuze does, who speaks about them in terms of the double: "The double is never a projection of the interior, it is on the contrary an interiorization of the outside" (*Foucault* [Paris: Minuit, 1986], p. 105, quoted by Elspeth Probyn, *Sexing the Self: Gendered Positions in Cultural Studies* [London: Routledge, 1993], p. 88).

50. Gertrude Stein, "Why I Like Detective Stories," in *Gertrude Stein: How Writing Is Written*, ed. Robert Bartlett Haas (Los Angeles: Black Sparrow Press, 1974), p. 148.

51. Stein uses recreation in an interview: "the idea of the recreation of the word. I took individual words and thought about them until I got their weight and volume complete and put them next to another word" (excerpt from "Gertrude Stein Talking—A Transatlantic Interview," in *Gertrude Stein: A Primer for the Gradual Understanding of Gertrude Stein*, ed. Robert Bartlett Haas [Los Angeles: Black Sparrow Press, 1971], p. 18).

I

Family vs. Female Wandering

1

Departing from Patrilinearity: The Deconstruction of the Family and *The Making of Americans*

TEXT, FAMILY, AND ORIGIN

Gertrude Stein's monumental *The Making of Americans* covers three generations of two (fictional) American families of the same ancestry. Although the first-person narrator promises to tell us the "story" of these families, and although the subtitle, "Being a History of a Family's Progress," suggests a continuous narrative of a constructive process, the book is about the deconstruction of the family in general and of the novel depicting family histories in particular. The book differs strikingly from American family sagas such as Allen Tate's *The Fathers*, Thomas Wolfe's *Look Homeward, Angel*, or Faulkner's *Absalom, Absalom!* Instead of telling a continuous story about the two families, the Herslands and the Dehnings, the narrator describes a great variety of the family members' traits in a discontinuous manner by giving us "portraits" of these individuals. The deconstruction of the family/families occurs on the level of narrative structure and within the family system.

The disrupted narration of a (patriarchal) family story already betrays a certain distrust of patrilinearity, as such stories are traditionally related in a chronological, more or less linear manner. In *Time and the Novel*, Patricia Tobin speaks of the "genealogical imperative" that "equates the temporal form of the classical novel . . . with the dynastic line that unites diverse generations of the genealogical family."[1] Of course we know that many novelists (mainly in the twentieth century) have revolted against linearity based on the family line. In James Joyce's *Ulysses*, for example, paternal authority is questioned and finally denied: Leopold Bloom has no son to continue the family line. If patrilinear narrative is robbed of the father, Roland Barthes's questions are understandable:

Death of the father would deprive literature of many of its pleasures. If there is no longer a father, why tell stories? Doesn't every narrative lead back to Oedipus? Isn't story-telling always a way of searching for one's origin?[2]

If "the father" disappears from the text, it loses its author-ity. The "death of the father" is therefore concomitant with the "death of the author."[3] But what are the characteristics of an authorless text? It no longer seems to have a fixed sub-jectivity at its center, identifying and claiming it. What then of the relationship between the text and its female author? So-called universal maxims and traditional concepts of writing do not necessarily—or very seldom—include the female because the female subject has never been in the center—how can it then become decentered? The question of female subjectivity has therefore become crucial in feminist criticism.

In her essay "Changing the Subject: Authorship, Writing, and the Reader," Nancy K. Miller convincingly argues that Barthes's dictum "the author is dead" cannot be applied to women writers without strong reservations: "But what does it mean to read (for) the woman writer when the Author is dead?"[4] Miller offers no clear-cut answer, but she argues forcefully that the female writing subject can only be described and defined with respect to the social text, that is, the "institution that authorizes and regulates most reading and writing."[5] Thus, the female writing subject is always constructed within an institution that may try to master it, but at the same time it can appropriate its own, "a woman's," language.[6] When describing a woman writer's text according to Barthes's notion of the "fatherless" (male) text, one must bear in mind the crucial fact that a woman writer has another relation to authority and institutions because of her position as a subject culturally and socially considered "the other"—the subject without authority.

In *The Making of Americans*, the patrilinear narrative is disrupted although the book is about the patriarchal family. Moreover, Stein explores themes that undermine the continuity of the family. I want to argue that the resulting decon-struction of the family only becomes "visible" if we read the text with a female writing subject in mind. A woman writer attempting to present a family history is confronted with paternal authority but also with her own female authorship.

The opening paragraph of *The Making of Americans* consists of two different parts, the first of which explicitly expresses filial rage:

Once an angry man dragged his father along the ground through his own orchard. "Stop!" cried the groaning old man at last, "Stop! I did not drag my father beyond this tree."[7]

This anecdote is from Aristotle's *Nicomachean Ethics* and should be a comment on people's acceptance of normal behavior as opposed to the unorthodox.[8] In the second part, strangely enough, the narrator emphasizes that the older we get the more tolerant we become as far as "our sins" (*MA*, p. 3) are concerned. It is difficult to establish a connection between these two parts of the prologue, as other critics have also pointed out.[9] Stein's marginal position as a lesbian writer may throw some light on this seemingly strange thematic combination of aggression and acceptance. Filial anger as expressed in the first part foreshadows resistance against patriarchal authority acted out and written down by Stein. But since this is considered typical of a son's behavior and Stein is a disobedient daughter, Aristotle's story does not apply to Stein. How can we interpret the Oedipal son's experience with regard to a female writer trying to rage against her father(s)? Lisa Ruddick suggests that Stein identifies with the angry son and that "her identity as a woman goes underground,"[10] but Stein does not necessarily identify with the son; on the contrary, being outside this patriarchal relationship, she tries to pretend that these "sins" are "harmless ones to own" (*MA*, p. 3) and thereby ignores her problematic position as a lesbian writer.

The following passage from the middle of the book is indicative of the author/narrator's problematic position toward creating/writing. The passage contains a crucial metaphor of the relationship between the narrator and her characters:

I am not content, I have not had it come out without pressing the description of Mr. Arragon the musician. It should come out of me without pressing without any straining in me to be pressing. Always each thing must come out completely from me leaving me inside me just then gently empty, so pleasantly and weakly gently empty, that is a happy way to have it come out of me each one that is making itself in me, that is the only way it can come to be content for me in me, it can come out fairly quickly very slowly with a burst or gently, any way it feels a need of coming out of me, but being out of me I must be very pleasantly most gently, often weakly empty, this one then Mr. Arragon is not so happily then out of me, he is then still there inside me, I will let him come again when he is more completely ready. (p. 586)

The narrator[11] is writing about the process of creating her characters. This process of creation is described as if the narrator were giving birth to a child. Writing is frequently compared to giving birth, but traditionally this literary topos has been (ab)used by male writers.[12] Here we have a female narrator, trying to "create" a family (history), who uses the metaphor of literary maternity. The narrator obviously has difficulties in "giving birth" to one particular character who does not come out as easily and smoothly as she wishes. She seems to have strong memories of other, more fulfilling births: she, as the "mother," must feel that she is relieved of a weight ("empty") and that her "womb" is relaxed and soft ("weakly gently"). Moreover, the "child" should come out when it is due and not before.

The metaphor of literary maternity used by Stein in a book about patriarchal family calls for particular attention. The narrator literally makes herself the mother of her characters, that is, she, the mother, is their procreator and nobody else. Yet, as this passage also reveals, "birth" is not always successful; "it is the coming out of [her] that has not been satisfactory" (p. 586) at all. Thus, even though the narrator perceives herself as the mother of her characters, at this point she does not have too much faith in her capability to give life to them. Does this mistrust already anticipate a possible death of the family? Indeed, she is even tempted to give up (pro)creativity: "And sometimes then I think it is all foolishness this I am writing and thinking and feeling and having as important being" (pp. 586–87). But she can reassure herself and overcome her doubts; "[she is] beginning again" (p. 587).

The metaphor of literary maternity can also be linked to another bodily process, that of excretion. First, Stein's vocabulary ("pressing," "empty" versus "full") hints at the process of releasing material that has filled the narrator. Second, Stein's repetitive style can be compared to the process of excretion: Retention and relief are characteristic of her paragraphs, which always retain something from the preceding one and yet signal a pleasure in releasing.[13] The psychoanalytical concept of anality emphasizes that the pleasure is evoked both through expulsion and retention. Stein's repetitive prose is playful and creates pleasure in a way similar to that in which children experience their libidinal organs (anus, urethra) during the so-called anal phase.[14]

Both metaphors for literary creativity—maternity and excretion—are linked with the body, in the first case exclusively with the female body. The body-text connection as theorized by Cixous (cf. my introduction) can be applied to Stein's writing. Cixous' well-known phrase "[m]ore body, hence more writing"[15] enables the female writer to experiment with language, as Cixous puts it, "to blow up the Law: an explosion henceforth possible and ineluctable; let it be done, right now, *in* language."[16] Kristeva's psychoanalytical notion of the *jouissance* that "breaks the symbolic chain, the taboo, the mastery"[17] is also pertinent to Stein's text. Furthermore, Kristeva comments on a striking aspect of anality that tends to deny sexual difference. Within the Christian context of the Virgin being impregnated by the Word, psychoanalysts report fantasies of anal pregnacy with—mainly—male analysands. Anal pregnancy leads to a "confusion of anus and vagina: in short, to a denial of sexual difference."[18] Interestingly, Lisa Ruddick, who expands on anality in *The Making of Americans*, mentions the possibility of Stein's "unconsciously marginalizing genital sexual difference"[19] because Stein focuses on people's "bottom nature" in order to differentiate between them:

Other kinds of natures are in almost all men and almost all women mixed up in them with the bottom nature of them, and this mixture in them with the amount they have in them of their bottom kind of nature in them makes in each one a different being from the many millions always being made like him. (p. 137)

Stein's combined use of the metaphors of maternity and anality indeed seem to point toward a refusal of clearly defined sexual difference, which, in turn, is necessary for a continuous line of (patriarchal) family.

With regard to anal pregnancy, Kristeva speaks of a homosexual economy in this context of Christian impregnation because she assumes that mostly male subjects have such fantasies; it is, according to Kristeva, a way of denying their difference from the mother. As a consequence, in this Christian order, a woman "should live and think of herself as a male homosexual."[20] This psychoanalytical interpretation can be related to Stein's homosexuality and the resulting problems that confronted her at that time and that may have influenced the composition of *The Making of Americans*: Trying to come to terms with her sexuality—above all, with her homosexuality—Stein creates a writing style that thematizes (sexual) difference and then tends to deconstruct it.

PIECES AND PORTRAITS OF PERSONS

The narrator's doubts and problems with regard to writing/creating/excreting are confided to the reader repetitiously. Her anxiety about not being able to describe each of her characters as "a whole" dominates many of their descriptions (e.g., pp. 327–28, 519–20, or 542–43). In some cases she feels a character as "a whole one in [her]" (p. 519), but when "it is coming out" it is only "in pieces" (p. 519, or p. 586) or "in fragments" (p. 519). Therefore, she begins again and again with the descriptions of her characters' many different traits. This perpetual return to beginnings entails many digressions and has an effect of discontinuity. These digressions together with the characters "in pieces" also seem to tear the family to pieces. It is interesting to note that Martha Hersland, who seems to be partly modeled on Gertrude Stein, is conceived of "as a whole" from the very beginning. But for her, too, disruption finally becomes real life: Her marriage to Phillip Redfern breaks up. Thus, pieces and fragments dominate the narrator's writing and the lives of her characters although she wishes to give birth to whole people. Fragments or pieces are also characteristic of the narrative line in *The Making of Americans*. Indeed, we can hardly speak of a line, since Stein gives us "portraits" of the single characters and not a linear story. In these literary portraits, Stein is concerned with the many different features of a human being, which calls for exact knowledge of an individual. To gain such knowledge, she creates classifications according to resemblance and difference. Resemblance and difference are key words in the composition of these portraits: "This being resembling, this seeing resemblances between those one is knowing is interesting, defining, confusing, uncertain and certain. You see one, the way of looking at any one in that one that is like some one, . . . it is confusing, too many people have pieces in them like pieces in this one" (p. 340). The pieces that persons have in common or that are different are not listed according to a conventional, sequential pattern, nor are they recognizable in a balanced way; one thing is as important as another: Composition is everything.

Stein uses a set of two basic categories that are, however, modified in each description:

As I was saying there are two general kinds of them, the resisting, the attacking kind of them. There are two general kinds of them, there are many very many kinds of these two kinds of them, there are many very very many mixings in every one of some of all the kinds of them, in some of some of both the general kinds of them I know this now and now I will describe more of it. (p. 345)

Relying on these two types of human nature, "resisting" and "attacking," Stein can observe differences and resemblances between people. In order to describe them, sometimes only slight modifications for each individual are necessary. These categories help Stein to describe a person's basic character because she

can rely on set characteristics. As she wants to describe so many different kinds
of people, her categories do not always satisfy her. One category, female-
ness/maleness, with stereotypical attributes, is quite conventional. This gender-
specific distinction was also used by Otto Weininger in his book *Sex and Character*, which Stein was reading in 1908 and which seems to have influenced her.
Weininger's book deals with problems of describing and explaining
psychological traits, and he presents a typology based on differences between
femaleness and maleness.[21] His prejudiced view of the sexes makes his book an
antifeminist tract because he considers the woman to be absolutely inferior to
the man, yet he states that bisexuality is inherent in every human being. The fact
that he attributes "a higher degree of development"[22] to a homosexual woman is
perhaps one reason why Stein recurred to Weininger's sexist book. Her concern
with this book is related to her attempt to come to terms with her own sexuality.
A hidden reference to homosexuality appears at the beginning of her book when
the narrator speaks about "Singulars" who are "misplaced" in society.
Especially if "singularity goes further and so gets to be always stronger, there
comes to be in it too much real danger for any middle class woman to follow it
farther" (p. 21).

As a woman who does not fit into the traditional pattern of a woman's role,
that is, being a homosexual and a writer, Stein had to face the problems of a
woman writer's status at the beginning of this century. Catharine Stimpson
speaks of the "feminization of the mind/body problem" with regard to Stein,
meaning "certain social and psychological questions that women had to confront
about the relationship of their minds to their bodies, "which is especially
pertinent to women of the intellectual elite.[23] Having left the United States,
settled in Paris, and acknowledged her homosexuality (though not in public),
Stein could not follow the patrilinear narrative; instead, she disrupted it and
created portraits in order to describe persons.

Portraiture is a genre Stein began to use while writing *The Making of Americans*, and she kept returning to it till the end of her life. The portraits she wrote
after *The Making of Americans* are usually shorter and are conceived as individual works.[24] In 1905/1906, while at work on *The Making of Americans*, Stein
was posing for a portrait by Picasso. It is well-known today that Stein and Picasso influenced each other's work, and that she was receptive to his Cubist
method, "a composition that had neither a beginning nor an end, a composition
of which one corner was as important as another corner."[25] This emphasis on
equal relations and nonhierarchical structures can hardly be a guideline for a
description of the patriarchal family. But a portrait of an individual person can
be composed according to such structural notions because the artist can focus on
this particular character. Stein explained why she began to compose portraits:

And so I am trying to tell you what doing portraits meant to me, I had to find out what it
was inside any one, and by any one I mean every one I had to find out inside every one
what was in them that was intrinsically exciting and I had to find out not by what they
said not by what they did not by how much or how little they resembled any other but I

had to find it out by the intensity of movement that there was inside in any one of them.[26]

In order to describe the whole of an individual, it is necessary to conceive of him or her in terms of a dynamic process, that is, movement. But this movement, as Stein saw it, is not related to time or memory; it is self-contained and not connected to any chronology or relational pattern.

Although at the beginning of her book the narrator states that "[w]e need only realise our parents, remember our grandparents and know ourselves and our history is complete" (p. 3), Stein does not submit to such a chronological pattern underlying the history of three generations. As a woman (writer) who had just literally separated herself from the land of her American (fore)fathers, Stein also separates herself from the fathers of the two families by taking the family apart. Displacing the father(s) means deconstructing the family.

By disrupting the family *and* the patrilinear narrative, a female writing subject is constructed because Stein creates "pieces" of her own. But what is the relation between these pieces and the disappearing family? The book's ending and its relation to the other parts can provide an answer.

The Making of Americans is divided into five sections, three of which are named after their main characters ("Martha Hersland," "Alfred Hersland and Julia Dehning," and "David Hersland"). The first part, which is untitled, introduces the two families, the Herslands and the Dehnings, but the narrator soon begins to dwell on various types of people and their human qualities. The last part, whose title is identical to the book's subtitle, "History of a Family's Progress," is not about any particular person or persons. In the three parts named after individuals, the marriages of the characters (Martha Hersland–Phillip Redfern and Alfred Hersland–Julia Dehning) break up; the protagonist of the third part, David Hersland, remains single and is "a dead one before he was a middle aged one" (p. 725). Thus, these three parts are overshadowed by final separations, by divorce or death.

Death is the topic, it seems, that prepares and introduces the last, and shortest, part of the book.[27] In the section on David Hersland's life and death the narrator emphasizes David's intellectual abilities, but she also refers to his inability to experience deep feelings or changes in his life:

Certainly he was not certain not always certain then that he was one being one feeling something. He was quite often quite certain that some being existing are ones being existing in feeling something. . . . He was one sometimes quite certain he was not one ever feeling and he was one who was quite certain that he was one who was one feeling enough to be a sad one and not feeling enough to have feeling being a thing that was being in him. (p. 845)

David Hersland is a "dead" person before he is "killed" by the author.[28] He is the only person with a personal name, while the others around him are called "ones" or "somes." Isolation and the inability to interact with others characterize the youngest son of the Hersland family. David Hersland's extreme retreat from real life into his mind cannot guarantee continuity or progress: "The making of

Americans becomes the unmaking of one American."[29] We can say not only that
the family dissolved but also that the American (male) hero is doomed to
disappear in this book.

It is significant that the narrative "I" also disappears in the course of the
chapter on David Hersland. Janice Doane suggests that without an "I" the narrative can flow without interruptions by the "I" (e.g., reflections on her narrative
mode).[30] The death of the narrative "I," however, can be connected with the
death of the family: After the descriptions of the disrupted marriages and the
lifeless existence of David Hersland, no person is described who can assure the
family line. As in Leopold Bloom's case, the family history must come to an
end. The female first-person narrator disappears as well; it seems as if she wants
to get away from the family. The narrative stance itself is a reflection of its own
narrative. The last part, ironically titled "History of a Family's Progress,"
epitomizes the impersonal, sexless, and abstract existence of the family.

In the last part of the book, no personal names or pronouns can be found at
all; "some," "some one," "any," and "any one" are the predominant subjects of
the sentences. These sentences explore many possibilities with respect to "being
in a family living":

Some being in a family living are certain of some such thing as being in any family
living. Some being in any family living are not certain of such a thing are not certain of
being in any family living being then existing, in their being then being living. Some
being in any family living are beginning some such thing are beginning being in any
family living. Some beginning being in any family living are not going on beginning
being in a family living. (p. 916)

Everything for "some" might go or not go. Although "family living" per se is
not denied, its existence is not concrete at all; the enumeration of so many possibilities is disconcerting. Although the first-person narrator has disappeared, we
feel the narrator's voice speaking to us ironically: She is the one who
remembers "some such thing [family living]" (p. 925), but at the same time she
annuls the validity of this statement because she is one among others who
remember—"*some* can remember something of some such thing" (p. 925, my
emphasis). The female narrator has become part of the impersonal "some." She
no longer addresses us directly, confiding her worries to us; on the contrary, she
leaves everything open with regard to "family living," and the reader must
decide for her- or himself which possibility might be true.

Family and death are now explicitly related to each other in many sentences
of the book's last pages. Again, no final decision about the continuity of the
family is articulated: people die and yet a family lives on; others may not have
any offspring, and thus "that family is not then existing" (p. 925). But what
counts is that "some are remembering some such thing [family living]" (p. 925).
The family can be remembered as "one being existing" (p. 925), although it has
no life of its own. Only the one who remembers is alive, namely the one
narrating "such thing."

The Making of Americans is also a book about the disappearance of a female first-person narrator. Having described herself as the mother of her characters in the middle of the book, she gives up "mothering" toward its end. The image of literary maternity is dissolved. This dissolution goes hand in hand with the deconstruction of the family. It is difficult to decide whether the dissolution of the family is the logical consequence of the disappearance of the narrator or vice versa; if the narrator can no longer mother her characters, they will not survive with a fixed identity. But if the family breaks up, the narrator conceived of as a mother can no longer fulfill her function. She is doomed to disappear like her male hero (David Hersland) of part four, her voice as "some" can only be heard faintly.

The pieces left over at the end of the book can hardly be called matriarchal because the narrator as mother has retreated and her characters have become genderless. Patriarchal authority is deconstructed, but it is not replaced by any female authority. Nevertheless, I do not think that the disruption of the family is a result of the female narrator's disappearance. As both patrilinear narrative *and* patriarchal family are disrupted, the female narrator must find a new voice. In *Tender Buttons*, written between 1910 and 1913,[31] an entirely new and different voice engages the reader in a dialogue: A definite female voice now speaks about things female.[32]

Stein's deconstruction of the family is not only connected with the function of the narrator. Her use of the "continuous present" also contributes to the questioning of linearity, the underlying principle of the family. In her lecture "Composition as Explanation," she describes how this particular present, which she also calls the prolonged present, was created:

In beginning writing I wrote a book called *Three Lives* this was written in 1905. I wrote a negro story called *Melanctha*. In that there was a constant recurring and beginning there was a marked direction in the direction of being in the present although naturally I had been accustomed to past present and future, and why, because the composition forming around me was a prolonged present. A composition of a prolonged present is a natural composition in the world as it has been these thirty years it was more and more a prolonged present. I created then a prolonged present naturally I knew nothing of a continuous present but it came naturally to me to make one, it was simple it was clear to me. . . . After that I did a book called *The Making of Americans* it is a long book about a thousand pages. Here again it was all so natural to me and more and more complicatedly a continuous present.[33]

The continuous present expresses each moment or event as new again; similar statements are repeated with slight modifications and thus presented as if in constant movement. The narrator must begin again and again with a description in order "to include everything."[34] The following description of Martha Hersland illustrates how Stein achieves a continuous modification by adding for example "sometimes" or "really," and thus changes similar statements and sentence structures:

Sometimes she was a little interesting to some one. She was never very interesting to her father or to any one knowing her in her young living. She was never really interesting to her father in her living. Later in his living she was always with him. In her young living as I was saying she was really not very interesting to any one. Always as I was saying she was the same whole one. When she was first a young woman she was a little interesting to some. She was never really very interesting to any one. Always, as I was saying, all her living, she was the same whole one. (p. 409)

Martha Hersland is described as a person whose surroundings are quite indifferent toward her. Indifference is mentioned in at least three different contexts: 1. her father's indifference toward her; 2. almost all the people of her daily life seem to be indifferent; 3. indifference after abortive sexual adventures ("When she was first a young woman she was a little interesting"; the sexual adventures are more explicitly referred to later in the book). The principle of the continuous present can be compared to the technology of the cinema: Just as moving pictures are simultaneously here and now, and always changing to the next frame, the present continuous presents a series of similar statements in movement to create a sense of continuous presence. Stein herself compares this process to film: "I was doing what the cinema was doing, I was making a continuous succession of the statement of what the person was until I had not many things but one thing."[35]

A description of three generations in this manner becomes a complicated undertaking. The use of the past, present, and future instead of Stein's continuous present would seem to be more reliable for describing a three-generation history of patriarchal family (grandfather-father-son) because these three traditional tenses express a chronological development. The continuous present, created by Stein because she had difficulties with chronological, patrilinear narrative, deconstructs the theme of *The Making of Americans*: The continuity of the family cannot be presented without past, present and future.

As outlined above, at the end the reader is left with the many descriptions of "somes" and "any ones." The impersonal generalization establishes a distance between reader and text; the intimate tone of the first-person narrator of the preceding sections is replaced by an uninvolved voice. The reader may ask him- or herself where the Steinian narrator is going.

What Stein has to say about the transition from *The Making of Americans* to *Tender Buttons* is significant. In "Portraits and Repetition" she explains that the composition of her portraits is dependent on "listening and talking" in order to present the here and now of a person. But besides listening and talking, looking became an important concern because she considered the visual aspect to be as crucial as the activities of hearing and talking; all three faculties can grasp moments of the now. But when describing human beings in words, one becomes involved with remembering; it is difficult to concentrate on one particular moment: "looking inevitably carried in its train realizing movements and expression and as such forced me into recognizing resemblances, and so forced remembering and in forcing remembering caused confusion of present with past and future time."[36]

Therefore, Stein concludes, she decided to write "portraits of things and enclosures that is rooms and places because [she] needed to completely face the difficulty of how to include what is seen with hearing and listening."[37] The portraits to which Stein refers are the "still lives" pictured in *Tender Buttons*.

In *The Making of Americans* Stein writes about the American family, yet her representation can only be deconstructive. The deconstructive means are creative in themselves: From the ashes of the patriarchal family, a new voice emerges and engages us in female "double-talk,"[38] as, for example, in *Tender Buttons*, where a female speaker addresses another female person in a very intimate and private tone. Among Stein's early plays, a number written shortly after *The Making of Americans*, similar dialogues take place. As in her portraits, Stein is eager to concentrate on the moment and does not want to rely on memory. According to Stein, in both portraits and plays she does not want to tell a story; in her portraits she tries "to tell what each one is without telling stories," and in her plays she focuses on "what happened without telling stories" (*LA*, pp. 121–22).

Stein's attempt at telling a family story has (ex)created[39] new forms, none of which can be restricted to one single genre. *Ida A Novel*—one of Stein's later works, which was explicitly given a generic label—is a book about female identity and textuality. Unlike *The Making of Americans*, the book constructs identity—and like *The Making of Americans*, deconstructs genre.

NOTES

1. Patricia Tobin, *Time and the Novel: The Genealogical Imperative* (Princeton, NJ: Princeton University Press, 1978), pp. 6–8.

2. Roland Barthes, *The Pleasure of the Text*, trans. Richard Miller (New York: Hill and Wang, 1975), p. 47. Janice Doane also refers to this quotation in her discussion of *The Making of Americans*, in *Silence and Narrative: The Early Novels of Gertrude Stein* (Westport, CT: Greenwood Press, 1986), p. 84.

3. See Roland Barthes, "The Death of the Author," in *Image-Music-Text*, trans. Stephen Heath (New York: Hill and Wang, 1977), pp. 142–48.

4. Nancy K. Miller, "Changing the Subject: Authorship, Writing, and the Reader," in *Feminist Studies/Cultural Studies*, ed. Teresa de Lauretis (Bloomington: Indiana University Press, 1986), p. 107.

5. Ibid., p. 112.

6. Miller gives an example of such a construction by focusing on Lucy Snowe in Charlotte Brontë's *Villette*, ibid., pp. 112–14, 116.

7. Gertrude Stein, *The Making of Americans* (New York: Something Else Press, 1966), p. 3. All page references in the text refer to this edition.

8. For Bridgman's comment on this passage, see Richard Bridgman, *Gertrude Stein in Pieces* (New York: Oxford University Press, 1970), p. 67.

9. See, for example, Janice L. Doane, *Silence and Narrative: The Early Novels of Gertrude Stein*, pp. 92–93; or Lisa Ruddick, *Reading Gertrude Stein: Body, Text, Gnosis* (Ithaca, NY: Cornell University Press, 1990), p. 58.

10. Ruddick, *Reading Gertrude Stein*, p. 59.

11. I follow Susan Sniader Lanser's suggestion "that the *noted* presence of a female name on the title page signals a female narrative voice in the absence of markings to the contrary" (Susan Sniader Lanser, *The Narrative Act: Point of View in Prose Fiction* [Princeton, NJ: Princeton University Press, 1981], p. 167). Lisa Ruddick distinguishes three different "voices" in *The Making of Americans*, each conveying a different consciousness. See Ruddick, *Reading Gertrude Stein*, p. 67.

12. The most well-known example is the sentence "You have heard, I suppose, that Thackeray is big with twenty parts, and unless he is wrong in his time, expects the first installment at Christmas." Elaine Showalter refers to this quotation by Douglas Jerrold, quoted in Kathleen Tillotson, *Novels of the Eighteen-Forties* (London, 1961), p. 39 n.; see Elaine Showalter, "Feminist Criticism in the Wilderness," in *Writing and Sexual Difference*, ed. Elizabeth Abel (Chicago: University of Chicago Press, 1982), p. 18.

13. Lisa Ruddick focuses on this aspect of anality in more detail; she also refers to Janine Chasseguet-Smirgel's essay "Perversion and the Universal Law," *International Review of Psycho-Analysis* 10 (1983): 293–301. Ruddick makes use of this psychoanalytical approach in order to show Stein's "anal-repetitive prose," which "forces all things to pass through something like an authorial body." See Ruddick, *Reading Gertrude Stein*, p. 82.

14. See also Ruddick, *Reading Gertrude Stein*, p. 79. Here one must also refer to Barthes, *The Pleasure of the Text*, trans. Richard Miller (New York: Farrar, Straus, and Giroux, 1975), in which he states: "Repetition itself creates bliss," p. 41. Ruddick also quotes this passage, p. 75.

15. Hélène Cixous, "The Laugh of the Medusa," in *New French Feminisms*, ed. Elaine Marks and Isabelle de Courtivron (New York: Schocken Books, 1981), p. 257.

16. Ibid.

17. Julia Kristeva, "About Chinese Women," in *The Kristeva Reader*, ed. Toril Moi (New York: Columbia Univeristy Press, 1986), p. 154.

18. Ibid., p. 147.

19. Ruddick, *Reading Gertrude Stein*, pp. 83–84.

20. Kristeva, "About Chinese Women," in *The Kristeva Reader*, p. 147.

21. For a discussion of Weininger's influence on Stein, see Leon Katz, "Weininger and *The Making of Americans*," in Michael Hoffman, ed. *Critical Essays on Gertrude Stein* (Boston: G. K. Hall, 1986), pp. 139–49.

22. Otto Weininger, *Sex and Character* (London: William Heinemann, 1906), p. 66.

23. Catharine R. Stimpson, "The Mind, the Body, and Gertrude Stein," *Critical Inquiry* 3, no. 3 (Spring 1977): 489.

24. In her definitions of Stein's literary portraits, Wendy Steiner does not consider *The Making of Americans* because, as she states, it is a narrative with fictionalized subjects. See Steiner, *Exact Resemblance to Exact Resemblance: The Literary Portraiture of Gertrude Stein* (New Haven, CT: Yale University Press, 1978), especially chapter two, "The Steinian Portraits: The History of a Theory," pp. 27–63.

25. Gertrude Stein, *Picasso* (London: B. T. Batsford, 1938; reprint, New York: Dover, 1984), p. 11. Page numbers refer to the reprint edition.

26. Gertrude Stein, *Lectures in America* (Boston: Beacon Press, 1985), p. 183.

27. See Richard Bridgman's comment on death and its significance in *The Making of Americans*. He refers to the Martha Hersland section, which contains crucial passages about the fear of death. In *Gertrude Stein in Pieces*, pp. 87–88.

28. Bridgman tells us Janet Flanner's story about Stein's killing the hero: "One day when she was writing *The Making of Americans*, she suddenly killed off the hero. She went to tell a friend and said, 'I've killed him.' 'My God, why?' 'I know all about him,'

she answered, 'and about them and about everybody in that story.'" In Gertrude Stein, *Two: Gertrude Stein and Her Brother and Other Early Portraits (1908–1912)* (New Haven, 1951), foreword by Janet Flanner, p. xiii; quoted in *Gertrude Stein in Pieces*, p. 86.

29. Clive Bush, "Towards the Outside: The Quest for Discontinuity in Gertrude Stein's *The Making of Americans: Being a History of a Family's Progress*," *Twentieth Century Literature* 24 (Spring 1978): 50. See also Lisa Ruddick's comment on "[h]ero-killing," which she connects with Stein's anger at her father and brother Leo, in *Reading Gertrude Stein*, p. 128. Ruddick, too, points out that the bourgeois family disappears.

30. Doane also maintains that David is modeled on Stein's brother Leo, from whom she was growing estranged around the time she was writing this part of the book. Some of Stein's own experiences with Leo seem to be described by the narrative "I" in the first part of this section. Doane therefore makes a connection between David's death and the end of Stein's shared life with her brother and the disappearance of the narrative "I." Janice Doane, *Silence and Narrative*, pp. 140–41.

31. Bridgman notes that it is not quite clear when exactly *Tender Buttons* (published in 1914), was composed. The Yale Catalogue gives the years 1910–1911 (p. 125). Pamela Hadas gives the dates 1910–1913 in "Spreading the Difference: One Way to Read Gertrude Stein's *Tender Buttons*," *Twentieth Century Literature* 24 (Spring 1978): 61.

32. For a feminist analysis of *Tender Buttons*, see Hadas, "Spreading the Difference"; Ruddick, "A Rosy Charm: Gertrude Stein and the Repressed Feminine," in *Critical Essays on Gertrude Stein*, ed. Michael Hoffman, pp. 225–40; or Chessman, *The Public Is Invited to Dance*.

33. Gertrude Stein, "Composition as Explanation," in *Selected Writings of Gertrude Stein*, ed. Carl Van Vechten (New York: Random House, 1962), pp. 517–18.

34. Gertrude Stein, *Lectures in America*, p. 159.

35. Gertrude Stein, *Lectures in America*, p. 176. For a more detailed discussion of the continuous present, see Doane, *Silence and Narrative*, pp. 122–44.

36. Gertrude Stein, *Lectures in America*, p. 188.

37. Ibid., p. 189.

38. See Neil Schmitz, *Of Huck and Alice: Humorous Writing in American Literature* (Minneapolis: University of Minnesota Press, 1983), p. 185.

39. Stein creates the word "excreate" in *Tender Buttons*, p. 496. The connection between creation and excretion is obvious.

2

Ida and Id-Entity

IDENTITY, ENTITY, PUBLICITY, AND MASTERPIECE

Ida A Novel is a book about identity and about the growing up of a young girl called Ida. Yet, Stein has not written a *Bildungsroman* with a female protagonist in quest of her identity. Rather, *Ida* can be called an "anti-*Bildungsroman*" because it does not depict the life of a young girl according to the generic model we know.[1] Instead, we witness the birth of Ida's "id-entity" and identity without a chronological presentation of the cultural and social influences on the protagonist. Identity and entity are both crucial in Stein's philosophy and are often mentioned together by Stein. The problem of identity in this book is linked with the issue of publicity, which was very much on Stein's mind at the time she wrote *Ida*. We know that she was interested in the role of the media in the affair of the Duke and Duchess of Windsor and about the ways publicity influences and shapes a personality. Her own role as a public figure after the success of *The Autobiography of Alice B. Toklas* also contributed to her ideas about publicity and identity.

The title, *Ida A Novel*, refers to a person and a book, "a novel." Thus, "Ida" connotes both book and character, and it is this connection that induced me to use Stein's concepts of identity and entity for this particular work. According to Stein, the first is intertwined with human nature, whereas entity belongs to the human mind. In her essay "What Are Master-Pieces and Why Are There So Few of Them"[2] she maintains that a masterpiece has to do with the human mind and not with human nature, which, in turn, is always related to identity. A masterpiece is an entity, "a thing in itself and not in relation" (p. 88). Human nature, on the other hand, is always related to something; it relies on memory in order to establish identity and is closely connected with "the business of living" (p. 88). The human mind has no identity and therefore it alone can create a masterpiece that is never based on remembering. The text—the entity text, so to speak—can be *about* human nature and thus, also about time and identity, but cannot be based upon them.

If we consider that *Ida* is both about the protagonist, Ida, and about the book, that is, the masterpiece, we can say that *Ida* has as its subject the creation of a person and of a masterpiece and its entity. Furthermore, the creation of the character's search for identity and the creation of the masterpiece are closely connected.

Stein's preoccupation with the figure of Ida in connection with issues of identity and literary creativity can also be found in other works. Ida appears for the first time as a protagonist in a short piece composed in 1937.[3] As in *Ida*, the question about the duality of Ida is raised. Is she two or is she one, or even more, as in *Doctor Faustus Lights the Lights* (1938), where the female protagonist is called "Marguerite Ida and Helena Annabel"? I suggest that the name "Ida" appealed to Stein because it implies the "id" of the Freudian notion of libidinal pleasure, which, however, contrary to Freud, is conceived as *the* leading principle in the process of identity.[4] As mentioned in the introduction, pleasure and *jouissance* can be found in many of Stein's texts and therefore it is not surprising that "Ida" and its psychoanalytical implications create pleasure, especially pleasure in and with language. Furthermore, the female suffix "a" feminizes the "id" of the unconscious and raises expectations with regard to a female protagonist and her identity.

Besides the psychoanalytical realm, we must also investigate the different genres in which "Ida" appears as a figure. The fact that on the front cover-page of the first copybook for Stein's draft the title "Ida, a twin" has been crossed out and replaced by "Ida, A Novel" suggests a link between "Ida" and literary text,[5] and, more specifically, a link between "Ida" and the generic label "novel." What are the implications of "Ida, a twin" and/or "Ida, A Novel" with respect to issues of identity and literary creativity? These are the questions to be addressed in this section.

THE BIRTH OF IDA

The book opens with the "baby born named Ida";[6] Ida arrives because the time seems right although the mother tries to prevent her birth, which is a very unusual thing to do. The analogy between childbearing and writing a book may throw some light on the mother's strange behavior. We recall that in *The Making of Americans* the childbirth metaphor was used by the narrator for the creation of one of her characters. The dominant tone of that passage, though, is one of doubt and mistrust toward creativity and/or writing, and that is connected with the way the two families in that book become fragmented. In *Ida*, ("real") childbirth also implies a certain anxiety on the part of the mother about giving life because she would rather keep the child inside, "but when the time came Ida came" (p. 7). The separation between mother and child cannot be prevented, that is, the creatress[7] does not have the control she has in *The Making of Americans*.

The childbirth passage in *Ida* can be read metaphorically if we remember that Ida is not only a character but also "a novel." Thus, Ida, the novel must be separated from its creatress, it seems, despite the fact that its author would like to keep it (inside). The relation between character and book is further complicated by the description of the birth: "And as Ida came, with her came her twin, so there she was Ida-Ida" (p. 7). As soon as Ida is born there is another, thus, Ida is not one but two, namely "Ida-Ida." Harriet Chessman, commenting on this passage, rightly points out that the two Idas "represent . . . self and other."[8] On the level of genre, that is, the novel, "Ida-Ida" implies that there is a companion to the first book. There is no such absolute thing as *one* book; it is always followed by another or, in terms of audience, it is heard, read, or listened to, and therefore no longer the same as when it was written. Writing as a process and writing as a product are the two ways of writing that Stein is so eager to combine.[9] We might say that on the metaphorical level the mother wants to prevent the birth of the child/book because she might be afraid of the reactions of the outer world, that is, the audience.

Thus, Ida-Ida, the hyphenated Ida so to speak, connotes not only the twins but also the possibility that Ida is a character *and* a book and, last but not least, that the book is not one book only but always more than one. Both character and book are intertwined and one does not exist without the other. The basis for this close relationship is language. Without the linguistic description ("Ida-Ida") Ida would not exist. Similarly, the book *Ida* is dependent on Ida the character because she triggers the search for identity and thus also for the book. Furthermore, Ida coming from her mother/creatress/author emerges as one whose language is still close to her mother tongue, that is, a language as yet untouched by the law of the father. It is in this context also that Harriet Chessman speaks of "Ida-Ida" as "baby talk, calling us back to the earlier world of intimacy in which such talk could be profoundly valued both for its expression of a link between self and m/other and for its delight in sound."[10]

Soon after the birth of Ida-Ida, her parents disappear without explanation, and Ida is left on her own. The first striking experiences she has are all connected with the male sex: "The first time she saw anything it frightened her. She saw a little boy and when he waved to her she would not look his way" (p. 8). Or: "Once she was lost that is to say a man followed her and that frightened her so that she was crying just as if she had been lost" (p. 9). Another episode involves "a man of course [who] jumped out from behind the trees and there was another with him" (p. 13). In all these passages Ida is exposed to male power; she is frightened by the phallic signifier ("The first time she saw anything it frightened her"). In order to protect herself Ida wishes she had a twin. The twin mentioned at her birth is never referred to again. Now, being older, Ida decides to have a twin so "nobody would know which one I [Ida] was and which one she was" (p. 13). As in a fairy tale or in a dream her wish becomes real ("And this did then happen" [p. 18]). "Real," though, in this novel can mean that the twin is only imagined in Ida's language, namely in her letters to her twin: "Ida often wrote letters to herself that is to say she wrote to her twin" (p. 18). Thus, Ida has become a twin and so there must be another twin also, but this "other" twin has no voice of her own.

Winnie, the name Ida gives her twin after she has won a beauty contest, is known by everybody, a fact that disconcerts Ida because some people just talk about her without obviously knowing her. This is reminiscent of Stein's own experience after the success of *The Autobiography of Alice B. Toklas*, when she became a celebrity people talked about; they did not read her other, more difficult works, which troubled Stein to such an extent that she had an enormous writing block. Similarly, Ida gets upset when she realizes that a man asks for Winnie although "[o]f course there was no Winnie" (p. 26) because Winnie is only an imagined (other) Ida. Ida even feels worse when another man, an officer, insists that she (Ida) is Winnie; she makes clear that "[h]er name was not Winnie it was Ida, there was no Winnie" (p. 29).

Ida's premonition that she is going to kill her twin although she has created her comes true: "they will call me a suicide blonde because my twin will have dyed her hair. And then they will call me a murderess because there will come the time when I will have killed my twin which I first made come. If you make her can you kill her" (p. 11). Another version of this passage appears in Stein's play *Lucretia Borgia. A Play*. The play is a typical Steinian play in the sense that it consists of four first acts and even an opera ("Lucretia Borgia. An Opera") that ends with this passage about the twin murder and one additional line: "One one one."[11] The play was written in 1938, when Stein was also working on *Doctor Faustus Lights the Lights* and *Ida A Novel*.[12] In all of these texts twinship is a central issue. In *Lucretia Borgia. A Play*, the twin Jenny must free herself of her twin Winnie whom she made come so she could write: "Jenny began to sit and write. Lucretia Borgia—an opera."[13] Killing her twin and beginning to write are closely related and one is suddenly reminded of Emily Dickinson's famous poem "My Life Had Stood—a Loaded Gun—" in which the female poet/speaker must first kill before she can be creative. In Dickinson's poem the destructive element necessary for the process of creativity is male, an animus so to speak.[14] Murdering the twin (who is always of the same sex in Stein's works) also has to do with the writer's persona, but it is definitely not an animus. On the contrary, the twin is part of the other (female) twin, but she can be killed because she is already an imagined one from the start: "If you made her [her twin] can you kill her. / One one one." Yet, the meaning of "can you kill her" is ambiguous because of the position of the auxiliary "can"; it may be read as a question and as an affirmative sentence with an inversion—not unusual in Stein's writing. Thus, the passsage can express some doubt about the "murder": How can you kill somebody who is imagined? I suggest that either reading is appropriate because the ambiguity is inherent in the fact that the twin *is* imagined, and thus we never know whether she can be killed by the one who made her.

The problem of identity, or multiple identities, cannot be solved. The line "one one one" implies more than one persona, but the pun on "won" can refer to the one who made the twin come and now has won because she has gotten rid of her other, public self and can now write again. I do not quite agree with Robert Bridgman who links the multiple identities in Stein's writing with Alice B. Toklas in *The Autobiography of Alice B. Toklas*, stating that Stein wrote through her but afterward never used her voice again and thus committed the murder.[15]

In terms of genre, it is a striking feature that in *Lucretia Borgia. A Play*, Jenny, who has several names, among them also Lucretia, begins to write an opera called "Lucretia Borgia." Thus, Jenny as author/creatress writes an opera and names it after her (other) self. The question of identity is based on naming, that is, writing, as it is at the beginning of *Ida* when Ida-Ida is born. As with the designation "Ida, A Novel," "Lucretia Borgia—an opera" connotes both a female person and a literary text. In Stein's "Identity A Poem" (1935) the relationship between identity and literary text is made even more explicit but nonetheless ambiguous. "Identity A Poem" begins with "Play 1" and continues with "Play 2" and three other plays ("Another Play").[16] The generic term "poem" in the title is challenged as soon as one reads (or hears) the next line ("Play 1"). In fact, the term "poem" never occurs again in the course of the piece, whereas *play* is a topic; the speaker comments on what a play is and presents various forms of plays. The title "Identity A Poem" does not seem to be relevant to the text that follows. Most of this text also appears in *The Geographical History of America*[17] (also written in 1935) but without the title "Identity A Poem." The piece titled "Identity. A Tale" with its subsections "A Poem," "A Conversation," "A Motto," "An Aphorism," and "Identity A Story"[18] presents "identity" in various explicitly labelled genres. I suggest that so many similar titles with different generic terms indicate how Stein grappled with identity and wanted to illustrate that identity, when written about, can be expressed through any genre, or that genre as such is irrelevant, and that identity is always created through the written text, that is, the masterpiece, the entity text.

TALKING, WANDERING, MARRYING

In *Ida A Novel*, the twin Ida has gotten rid of her other twin, but she is not a whole "one" yet. The search for her identity continues after she has "murdered" Winnie. It is not coincidental that following the murder Ida begins to travel. As soon as people mention Winnie, Ida leaves. Roaming about, Ida also contemplates, for the first time, getting married. After thinking about it she decides not to; instead, she "decided that she was just going to talk to herself" (p. 43). Thus, talking is an option to marrying, to being together with another one. Again it is through language that Ida tries to enter a relationship, even if it is only a relationship between her(self) speaking and her(self) listening.

Nevertheless, after a while Ida does marry, but the focus of marriage is not, as in most traditional narratives, on union and progeny.[19] Ida is still the center and in search of her own self. The husbands that follow after the first one either disappear or are left by Ida. In fact, Ida "went all around the world" and "everything she saw interested her" (p. 51). The patriarchal institution of marriage does not seem to promote the idea of a "whole," of a self that is complete. Although Ida always tries again, she finally decides to rest in Washington. Resting for Ida does not necessarily imply leisure; like talking and listening to herself, resting means turning inward, but it does not exclude the others around her. It is part of Ida's quest, which does not consist of any aggressive, heroic activity. Yet, for her it means that she "was busy resting" (p. 88).

Ida is married once more; she becomes Mrs. Gerald Seaton before she meets Andrew, who makes her "more Ida" (p. 90). The following passage about her life as Mrs. Gerald Seaton depicts the emptiness and estrangement in this marriage:

They talked together at least some time every day and occasionally in the evening but that was all and when they talked she called out to him and he did not answer and he called out to her and mostly she did not answer but they were sometimes in their home together. Anyway they were married and had been for quite some time. (p. 88)

All of Ida's husbands, except Andrew, lack the ability to listen. Instead, most of them talk, but not to themselves as Ida does. As these husbands appropriate language without letting Ida participate, she leaves them—and patriarchal language—behind. Only Andrew lets her be "Ida itself" (p. 90).

I-DA AND AND-(R)YOU

Like Ida in her imagined life as a twin, Andrew is also "one of two" (p. 87), but he seems to be a real twin: "He was so completely one of two that he was two" (p. 87). Yet, the relationship between him and Ida changes his identity: Since he made her "more Ida," "Ida changed Andrew to be less Andrew" (p. 90). Their relationship is based on equality and not on any hierarchical principle: If there is more of Ida's personality in their relationship, then consequently there is less of Andrew's. Yet, their activities seem to be interchangeable—the place they occupy is sometimes Ida's, sometimes Andrew's. Even their sex seems to change, that is, Ida becomes Andrew and vice versa: "You see there was he it came to be Andrew again and it was Ida" (p. 95). Harriet Chessman speaks of a "rich confusion of gender" that "replaces the hierarchical male-female 'marriage' with the profoundly democratic model of twins."[20] Moreover, place, person, gender, and meaning are unfixed; there is no center from which an orientation would be possible. Stein's advice from *Tender Buttons*, "Act so that there is no use in a centre,"[21] is heeded by Ida and Andrew, but also by the author of *Ida A Novel*. The reader/listener must equally be responsive to this attitude because he or she cannot rely on any center or direction. But this attitude opens up an enormous amount of possibilities; the effects of decentralization and decentering "are no longer understood as chaos or absence—the opposite of presence—but as a marvelous expansion, a multiplicity of independent centers."[22]

The union between Ida and Andrew has been compared to Gertrude Stein's marriage to Alice B. Toklas.[23] Like Ida, who is "almost married to Andrew" (p.

11), Stein was "almost" married to Toklas. Their lesbian relationship was based on "sameness" in the sense that both were of the same sex. In the section of this book on *The Ladies' Voices*, I argue in more detail that lesbian subjectivity is not determined by binary difference between subject and object as with phallogocentric subjectivity. It is not surprising, therefore, that Andrew is described as follows: "Andrew although he was different was the *same*" (p. 150; my emphasis). Difference and sameness are characteristic of the relationship between Ida and Andrew; walking and talking about their walks becomes an activity that is essential for both in the same way: "Every day she talked the same way and every day she took a walk and every day Ida was there and every day she talked about his walk, and every day Ida did listen while she talked about his walk. . . . [I]t can be very pleasant to listen every day to him talk about his every-day walk" (p. 95).

The dialogic form of talking and listening creates pleasure for Ida and Andrew. It is important that these activities are alternating, thus not restricted to one of the two. The pleasure aroused is rooted in language with two equal partners/speakers. This erotic dimension, *jouissance*, can playfully be located in the names of Ida and Andrew: "I" is "da" and engages in a dialogue "and are you?" ("And-r-ew?").

Apart from the fact that Ida and Andrew are "the same" like Stein and Toklas, there are other indications that *Ida* is an autobiographical text.[24] The story about a "life with dogs" (pp. 96–106) in the second half of *Ida* was written separately as "My Life With Dogs" and inserted later.[25] Ida as a first-person narrator tells us about the many dogs she has had; we know that they actually were Stein's because of the familiar names (e.g., Basket and Polybe). Stein obviously did not want to conceal that this story was originally a self-contained piece. This "story" easily fits into the novel, which, as we know, cannot follow any linear development according to Stein. This kind of composition is not unusual for her work; she often uses a whole or parts of a piece in various texts. Thus, this combination of explicitly autobiographical texts and more or less fictive texts contributes to the dissolution of generic boundaries. Moreover, this combination in *Ida A Novel* subverts the form of the *Bildungsroman* because Ida as its protagonist can also be the narrator (and voice) of another story, or because the *Bildungsroman* is disrupted by other stories that contain autobiographical pieces. One such story told to Ida and Andrew is about superstition. Another is about a woman writer who had written "a lovely book but nobody took the lovely book nobody paid her money for the lovely book . . . and she was poor and they needed money oh yes they did she and her lover" (p. 124). Finally somebody is sorry for the woman writer and gives her a little money. In the spring she goes out, still wishing for money, and meets a cuckoo that sings to her: "and she sang cuckoo cuckoo to it, and there they were singing cuckoo she to it and it to her. Then she knew that it was true and that she would be rich and love would not leave her and she would have all three money and love and a cuckoo in a tree, all three" (p. 125). Stein's own situation as an unpublished writer (until the popular success of *The Autobiography of Alice B.*

Toklas) immediately comes to mind. Moreover, the story of the cuckoo emphasizes a crucial aspect of Stein's works, namely the dialogue, speaking and listening. Neil Schmitz's comment on this passage is to the point: He calls the woman writer and the cuckoo "two experts in double-talk."[26] We might say that Stein and the cuckoo share the capability of engaging in a never-ending dialogue of sounds (words) with a repetitive but nevertheless poetic and playful quality.

These autobiographical pieces are linked to Ida and her search for identity because they illustrate that digression, repetition, and exaggeration belong to "Everybody's Autobiography," be it Ida's or be it "Ida's Novel." Stein shows us that an account of Ida's life cannot have a definite narrative line; how could a narrative line be in concordance with the wanderings of such a person as Ida? Moreover, a form to express Ida's constant desire to go on and to rest at the same time is bound to be open, multiplying, and even contradicting.[27]

For the narrator of Ida's story, contradictions belong to her language, and even the structure of her sentences contain seemingly contradictory sequences. The following example is an attempt to linguistically probe the relationship between "happen" and "begin" with regard to Ida:

When something happens nothing begins. When anything begins then nothing happens and you could always say with Ida that nothing began. . . . That was the way it was nothing did happen everybody talked all day and every day about Ida and Andrew but nothing could happen as neither the one of them or the other one ever did begin anything. It is wonderful how things pile up even if nothing is added. (pp. 150–51)

The narrator establishes a relationship between "to happen" and "to begin" assuming that "begin" may be a consequence of "happen," but she immediately denies it. She proves her argument by partly reversing the first two sentences, that is, by replacing "happens" with "begins" and "something" with "anything." In the third sentence the logical relationship between "to happen" and "to begin" is reversed again, namely it is implied that "to begin" is a consequence of "to happen" ("but nothing could happen as neither the one of them . . . did begin anything"). This kind of linguistic "experiment" is void of the logic we are accustomed to and rely on in order to communicate because it is based on the reversal of *words* only and not of their meanings. The signifier switches places regardless of its signified, and yet, new meaning is created all the same or, more precisely, multiple meaning is achieved. Both "[n]o and yes" (p. 154), as the narrator says toward the end of *Ida*, are possible. Whatever position the words occupy, they are connected in such a way as to create a meaning. Indeed, "[i]t is impossible to put them [words] together without sense," as Stein explains in an interview talking about "the recreation of the word."[28]

At the end of the book, Ida's search for identity does not end, since she goes on and does not go on (cf. p. 154), and as "she goes out she comes in" (p. 154). According to Stein, identity cannot be the basis for an entity text, that is, a masterpiece; this masterpiece can only be about identity without the help of memory because remembering belongs to human nature and this, in turn, is related to identity. Since Ida does not rely on time, or memory, she moves within the realm of the human mind. We can say that Ida is an entity herself; like a masterpiece she belongs to the present, to the here and now without being defined by beginning or end. As an early critic, Donald Sutherland, aptly puts it, "her simple existence has become her essence."[29]

Ida's self-awareness is further connected with this issue of entity and masterpiece by what the narrator calls "genius." Stein had very definite notions about genius ("one who is at the same time talking and listening," *LA*, p. 170), and it is not a coincidence that Ida is described as one who "knew she had her genius" (p. 94). She has her genius because she can always do both, going out and going in, moving and resting, talking and listening: "[S]he [Ida] talked as if she knew that Ida knew how to listen" (p. 95). Since she knows so absolutely that she has her genius, she can be together with Andrew without fear of losing her entity, her autonomy.[30] It is not surprising that the last word of the book is "yes," it not being possible to distinguish whether this is Ida's word or the narrator's, that is, the book's: Ida and the book become one and whole in the same way that Ida becomes more Ida through Andrew.[31] The dialogue "I da" "And(r)ew?" ("and are you?") has been given a further piece of dialogue—the last word of the masterpiece. But it is not a final word because it is not determined; the "yes" can also be the yes of the reader who will continue the dialogue.

The emphasis on dialogue or, more precisely, on "I" and "A" (for Andrew) with the connecting "D" in the middle is further illustrated by the graphic arrangement of the title *Ida* in the Random House and Vintage edition:

$$D$$
$$I \quad A$$

We can also read the three letters by beginning with the "D," thereby composing the word "DIA" meaning "through," "across," or "between."[32] All these meanings are implied in dialogue, entity, identity, and masterpiece as they appear in Stein's *Ida A Novel*.

Unlike *The Making of Americans*, which finally is a book about the death of a family, *Ida A Novel* is about the birth of a textual female "I." Whereas in the former the family is dissolved into the impersonal "somes" and "any ones," in the latter the autonomous "I" of Ida is being joined by another, Andrew, without threatening Ida's entity. Both Ida the character and Ida the novel are more than one in the sense that they are not determined by either fixed character descriptions (Ida) or by a story or plot line. The latter is also true for *The Making of Americans*, but it seems that at that stage of Stein's life and literary career, a creation of such a strong character as Ida was not possible. The patriarchal family had to be deconstructed first before a female "I" could state "I da" without reference to the past or future; thus, the present is created in the character and in the entity text. It does not matter whether it is a novel or any other form of text; genre itself becomes irrelevant.

In the next part I investigate the depth to which this conclusion is also true for Stein's plays and operas.

NOTES

1. Cynthia Secor calls *Ida* a "Bildungsroman," although she, too, emphasizes that there is "no conventional maturation and no crises of identity." See Secor, "*Ida*, A Great American Novel," *Twentieth Century Literature*, Gertrude Stein issue, 24 (Spring 1978), no. 1: 97. Neil Schmitz also calls *Ida* a Bildungsroman. See *Of Huck and Alice: Humours Writing in American Literature* (Minneapolis: University of Minnesota Press, 1983), p. 229. He speaks of a "disembodied bildungsroman" (p. 235).

2. Gertrude Stein, "What Are Master-Pieces and Why Are There So Few of Them," in *What Are Masterpieces and Why Are There So Few of Them* (Los Angeles: Conference Press, 1940), pp. 81–95.

3. Richard Bridgman gives an informative account of the various pieces in which "Ida" appears. See Bridgman, *Gertrude Stein in Pieces* (New York: Oxford University Press, 1970), pp. 305–7. Shirley Neuman comments on the several drafts of the opening of *Ida* and on the other pieces in which "Ida" appears, including *Doctor Faustus Lights the Lights*, in her "'Would a Viper Have Stung Her If She Had Only Had One Name?' *Doctor Faustus Lights the Lights*," in *Gertrude Stein and the Making of Literature*, ed. Shirley Neuman and Ira B. Nadel (London: Macmillan, 1988), pp. 168–93.

4. Chessman also comments on this emphasis on the "id" as opposed to the Freudian notion. See Chessman, *The Public Is Invited*, p. 169.

5. I acknowledge Harriet Chessman for providing me with this information about the manuscript. See Chessman, ibid., p. 230 n. 9.

6. Gertrude Stein, *Ida A Novel* (New York: Random House, 1968), p. 7. All page references in the text refer to this edition.

7. Julia Kristeva coins this word. See "Women's Time," in *The Kristeva Reader*, ed. Toril Moi, p. 205.

8. Chessman, *The Public Is Invited*, p. 168.

9. I shall comment on this aspect in the chapter on *Four in America* in which Stein explains these two ways of writing.

10. Chessman, *The Public Is Invited*, p. 169.

11. Gertrude Stein, "Lucretia Borgia. A Play," in *Reflection on the Atomic Bomb, vol. I of the Previously Uncollected Writings of Gertrude Stein*, ed. Robert Bartlett Haas (Los Angeles: Black Sparrow Press, 1975), p. 137.

12. See Shirley Neuman's informative chronology in her "'Would a Viper,'" p. 191.

13. Ibid.

14. For the complex relationship between the animus and the poet/speaker, see Albert Gelpi's illuminating essay "Emily Dickinson and the Deerslayer: The Dilemma of the Woman Poet in America," in *Shakespeare's Sisters: Feminist Essays on Women Poets*, ed. Sandra Gilbert and Susan Gubar (Bloomington: Indiana University Press, 1979), pp. 122–32.

15. Bridgman, *Gertrude Stein in Pieces*, p. 305. Yet, Bridgman adds that the multiple identities "might refer to the several psychological roles Gertrude Stein detected within herself over the years."

16. Gertrude Stein, "Identity A Poem," in *What Are Masterpieces*, pp. 71, 73, 74. Ulla Dydo provides us with the interesting information that Stein sent this text to Donald Vestal, a puppeteer, whom Stein had met on the street in Chicago. He asked her to write

a play for his marionettes and she then sent him this text. See *A Stein Reader*, ed. Ulla Dydo (Evanston, IL: Northwestern University Press, 1993), p. 588.

17. Gertrude Stein, *The Geographical History of America*, pp. 63–78.

18. Gertrude Stein, *Painted Lace and Other Pieces [1914–1937]*, vol. v of the Yale Edition of the Unpublished Writings of Gertrude Stein (New Haven, CT: Yale University Press, 1955; reprint, New York: Books for Libraries Press, 1969), pp. 69–71.

19. Cynthia Secor emphasizes this aspect in "*Ida*, A Great American Novel," p. 98.

20. Chessman, *The Public Is Invited*, p. 190.

21. Stein, *Tender Buttons*, p. 498.

22. Trinh T. Minh-ha, "*L'Innécriture:* Un-Writing/Inmost Writing," in *When the Moon Waxes Red* (London: Routledge, 1991), p. 142. This essay was originally published in French in *French Forum*, 8, no. 1 (January 1983).

23. Secor, "*Ida*, A Great American Novel," p. 106; and Chessman, *The Public Is Invited*, p. 232, n. 19.

24. Chessman also makes this point, *The Public Is Invited*, pp. 230–31, n. 12.

25. See Bridgman, *Gertrude Stein in Pieces*, p. 309n.

26. Schmitz, *Of Huck and Alice*, p. 235.

27. Ellen Berry makes a similar point although referring to *Ida* as a *melodrama* and its implication of female desire: "[Stein] suggests at least one solution to melodrama's central ideological contradiction by shifting the forms that ensure the containment of female desire or demand that it be expressed as an impossible contradiction within processes of representation" (Berry, *Curved Thought*, p. 175).

28. Stein, "A Transatlantic Interview 1946," p. 18. Although Stein speaks about her "middle period," that is, the period during which she wrote portraits, this statement is pertinent to all of her writings.

29. Donald Sutherland, *Gertrude Stein: A Biography of Her Work* (New Haven, CT: Yale University Press, 1951), p. 158.

30. It is interesting to note that in Stein's short piece "Identity. A Tale," in the subsection "A Conversation," a short dialogue takes place between Sweet William and Lilian about who and what a genius is. In the first section we learn that "Sweet William had his genius." Irony rings through the whole "Conversation" because Lilian does not seem to give Sweet William the positive answer he wishes for, namely the affirmation that he is a/the genius. It is implied that Lilian equally has *her* genius. See "Identity. A Tale," in *Painted Lace*, pp. 69–70.

31. Harriet Chessman therefore calls Andrew "a twin who may be called into existence simply by his name." *The Public Is Invited to Dance*, p. 196.

32. See also bp Nichol's comment on the layout of *Ida*; he mentions another reader's observation that "both the I & the A achieve their singularity & the D is brought into question." Then the letter "L" (for Love) is added:

D L

I A

In this two-letter configuration "D is Death . . . & L is Love." See "When the Time Came," in *Gertrude Stein and the Making of Literature*, ed. Neuman and Nadel, p. 208.

II

Voices and Votes
in Plays and Operas

3

Stein Plays:
A Circular Play (1920)

The two book-length studies dealing with Stein's dramatic work demonstrate how difficult it is to classify Stein's plays. Betsy Alayne Ryan and Jane Palatini Bowers, the authors of these books, develop quite different approaches toward Stein's plays. Ryan is mainly interested in the "performance text," whereas Bowers relies on the "dramatic text" to explore and analyze the metadramatic issues.[1] I suggest that both views are compatible and should even be combined when discussing the Stein texts, which comment on dramatic conventions and the theatricality of a play but must also be "read" as performance texts, in other words, as if they were live performances that we *see* or could see. *A Circular Play* with its subtitle *A Play in Circles* illustrates Stein's ideas on drama as expressed in her more theoretical writing in *Lectures in America*. Although her lecture on "Plays" was written many years after *A Circular Play*, it contains essential observations that are also pertinent to *A Circular Play*. Critics should not read Stein's comments on her own work as straightforward explanations because they themselves need clarification and commentary; nevertheless, they provide us with insights into Stein's way of thinking and writing.

Stein's approach to plays is influenced by her general concern about time and about the ways human beings are affected by it. It is not surprising that her starting point is a very concrete situation: She describes her experience at the theater watching a play, which made her nervous because "your emotion concerning the play is always either behind or ahead of the play at which you are looking and to which you are listening. Your emotion as a member of the audience is never going on at the same time as the action of the play."[2] The cause of this lack of combinatory capabilities lies, according to Stein, partly in the relation between seeing or hearing and feeling: One's emotions concerning movements, voices, music, clothes, etc., are constantly interrupted because the play moves on, and one has to cope with a new scene that triggers new emotions. Stein uses the concept of the landscape, which fits her idea of not moving, of "stillness":

I felt that if a play was exactly like a landscape then there would be no difficulty about the emotion of the person looking on at the play being behind or ahead of the play because the landscape does not have to make acquaintance. You may have to make acquaintance with it, but it does not with you, it is there and so the play being written the relation between you at any time is so exactly that that it is of no importance unless you look at it. (*LA*, p. 122)

The problem of time with regard to perceptions and emotions is linked with the general "problem of anybody living in the composition of the present time" (*LA*, p. 104). To present a scene in the actual present without referring back to a past moment that could influence the present scene became one of the main concerns of Stein's literary production. Many of her plays thematize the problem of presenting the "present" moment on stage. *A Circular Play* is one of these attempts to express immediacy both on stage and in language.

The title already implies that this play will have no beginning or end because we can never tell where and *when* a circle begins. The adjective "circular" emphasizes the idea that the play to be read, heard, or seen will not follow any linear pattern. The subtitle *A Play in Circles* opens up the spatial dimension: The announced play not only assumes circularity but also proclaims movement in circles, which from the first line are reminiscent of children's play: "First in a circle."[3] The following line, "Papa dozes mamma blows her noses" (p. 139), has the ring of a nursery rhyme, enhancing the idea of an easygoing atmosphere among children at play. Yet, this playful world in a (first) circle is not turning like a merry-go-round; it seems to be a circle pushed off-center because Stein alludes to a shattered world in the next lines, namely to World War I ("Then suddenly there was an army" [p. 139]). With the mention of Mildred Aldrich there is a further, more explicit and more autobiographical allusion to this war; Mildred Aldrich, a close friend of Stein and Toklas, remained in her house on a hilltop near the Marne while the battle was going on.

Remarks about disorder, chaos, or war are often made together with an enumeration of seemingly static items: "Coal and wood. / Hat blocked" or "Little silver clasp for necklace" (p. 140). The combination of inanimate objects with personal or more emotional passages creates a kind of circle through sheer repetition during the course of the play except that the combinations themselves are always different. It is as if Stein wants to present an inner and outer circle of human existence. Indeed, the inner and outer circles can also be linked with the inside of the mind (war) and the outside of a performance (objects). Renée Riese Hubert, one of the few critics to have commented on this play, sees the circle as "a spatial order, either inside the mind or outside in the arena of the performance."[4] But Hubert, too, emphasizes that the spatial order does not suggest a fixed center at all. Stein seems to explore a certain word or attitude and then all of a sudden it is dismissed and a new word or mini-topic is introduced. The following lines show this kind of exploring or encircling:

Stop being thundering.
I meant wondering.
He meant blundering.
I have been mistaken.
No one is so certain.
She is certain.
Certainly right.
Can I be so sorry.
How can I turn around. I will leave it to her to decide how to arrange it.
                                        Circle Hats.
My color.
Their color.
Two
One
Two won.
I can think so quickly.
Silent and thoughtful. Crimson rambler and a legion post
legion, a poor post legion. Crimson rambler or star. (p. 140)

I suggest that the first three lines belong together because of the onomatopoetic use of the gerund, whereas the fourth line introduces the semantic field of "mistaken" and "certain," which ends with the long sentence ("to arrange it"). The third part deals with "color" and puns on "two" and "one." "Two won," possibly referring to "my color" and "their color," could express the elimination of a kind of opposition or contrast. The line "I can think so quickly" is striking in two ways: It is self-reflective as far as the first-person speaker is concerned and thus could be read as a comment on the pun. The first-person speaker herself[5] is surprised and pleased by her linguistic play. Furthermore, this kind of self-reflection in a play undermines the opposition between the dramatic realm of the *spoken* and what a character/narrator *thinks*. The last two lines of the quotation contain both references to color ("Crimson rambler") and to "thinking"; "a legion" takes up again the theme of war. "Crimson rambler" may allude to red climbing roses; "rambler" can also refer to someone wandering both literally and verbally. In *Tender Buttons*, shades of red such as crimson, pink, or rosy also abound, but I think that the last line remains fairly cryptic.

These "circles" are punctuated by titles such as "Circle Hats," "Circles," "In a circle," "The Idea of a Circle," "Circle One," "Circle Two." These markings of division *seem* to structure the play but, in fact, they question the principle of structuring, of dividing a play into acts or scenes. Most of these titles are interchangeable and could even be part of the main body of the text. Therefore I do not agree with Betsy A. Ryan who claims that the circles "serve as virtual scene divisions, there being a specific character to each circle which is not continued into the next circle."[6] The "circle" titles are indeed circular because some of them are repeated in slightly modified versions such as "Leave a Circle" and "Leaves or a Circle" (p. 143), or "The Third Circle" (p. 139) and "Circle Three" (p. 143). The verbal play of these modifications sensitizes the reader toward these words and their possible combinations. Meaning is presented as a multiple, ever-changing process before the eyes and for the ears of the reader or spectator.

Since there is neither a linear plot nor a fixed group of characters, more attention is focused on the words and pieces of conversation. The reader or spectator recognizes many clusters of everyday speech, yet he or she can never follow a progressive line and is constantly taken aback by new turns or, as it were, by new circles of words or phrases. Yet, within the seemingly disconnected phrases a "plot" can sometimes be detected, expressed in unusual verbal combinations such as "thought" and "receipt":

> An inner circle.
> And inner circle again. Do tease me. Nose kisses and thirds. I have been deceived. No you have been refused. I have refused ten spots as one. But not as ten. But not as too. Dear thought and receipt. (p. 142)

I read this passage as a dialogue between two persons who are close ("Nose kisses") to each other and are now engaged in a dispute. The word "Caesar" and "Caesars" in the preceding line may refer to the sexual realm of this relationship, as "Caesar" occurs in many of Stein's texts and often alludes to a woman's breasts or orgasm (see Chapter 4 on *Ladies' Voices*). "[S]pots" may be an allusion to menstruation or defloration as in *Tender Buttons*, where "spots" and "stains" have this connotation.[7] The dispute is not presented as a straightforward dialogue with clearly recognizable speakers, but expresses the contrary views ("ten spots"—"not as ten") through the words "thought" and "receipt." These words belong to entirely different semantic fields, yet in this context they refer to the essential problem of human communication, namely the big difference between what one *thinks* (in his or her inner circle) and how it is received by the outside world after the *thought* has been externalized. The frequent consequence, namely a misunderstanding between the speakers, is expressed by "deceived" and "refused." This miniscene dramatically illustrates the difficulties of dialogue by circling a few essential words and by demonstrating possible consequences of their use.

In contrast to traditional dramatic dialogue, the speaker and the addressee do not have fixed lines except for the few that appear in question answer form (e.g., "Can you. . . / Yes I see. . .," pp. 150–51). The verbal indeterminacy brings the speakers closer together because the words and their utterers are interchangeable; there is no dividing line between them—they become one "I" or, as Stein puts it in *The Geographical History of America*, "I am II."[8] This kind of dialogue only lasts for a moment; it does not develop and has no continuity. It does not relate to other pieces of dialogue in the course of the play. The immediacy of the words is enhanced because they do not refer back to a preceding scene, even though certain words or modified combinations turn up again. The reader's or spectator's emotional entanglement is avoided because he or she must focus attention on the present use of the words and sounds. The "meaning" in process never remains the same—it is indeed in circulation all the time. Thus, the performance must become as much a changing process as the words themselves, and one can only agree with Hubert who sees a close relationship between performance and the writing process:

Not only do Stein's manipulations of drama as a generic form of writing efface the barrier between the playwright and the critic, but by dint of persistent displacements they turn words, particularly those implying circularity, into performers. Indeed, Stein has made performance and the writing process interchangeable.[9]

This comment is especially pertinent to the way Stein plays with the "identity" of the speakers. The reader cannot fix their identities, their names can seldom be attributed to a fixed, stable character. According to Hubert, "Mrs. Persons" (p. 148) is a case in point: Her name represents a personification of "everybody" and opens up theatrical possibilities because "Mrs. Persons" could characterize many different persons throughout the play. But it also makes a fixed identity impossible. Names such as Alice (mentioned several times) or Mildred Aldrich can be identified to a certain extent because they belong to the circle around Gertrude Stein or have obvious referents, and thus carry associations for some readers/spectators. But most names in *A Circular Play* cannot be attributed to specific speakers by an audience and undermine the conventional notion of the dramatis personae.

There seem to be various first-person speakers, but it is never really clear who is speaking when. This unstable distribution of voices leaves ample freedom to a director of the play. It also emphasizes the dialogic form without fixing the speaking partners. The dialogues assigned to characters are pertinent to drama, yet Stein radically challenges both the form of dialogue and traditional casting. The resulting openness enables the reader/spectator to focus on the present moment because he or she does not have to follow a continuous piece of dialogue or to remember a certain cast.

The speakers' tone is usually very personal and conversational; we seem to be listening to a group of people on very familiar terms with each other. The soft and intimate tone of some of the speakers (or of one and the same?) conveys the idea that they are addressing a female partner/friend who might be their lover and with whom they share their daily life:

A circlet of kisses.
Can you kiss to see.
Some see.
Can you kiss me.
I see.
Can you hear of kissing me.
Yes I see where you can be.
Do I sound like Alice.
Any voice is resembling.
By this I mean when I am accustomed to them their voices sound in my ears.
. . .
Circles are candy.
Irregular circles.
Can you think with me.

I can hear Alice.
So can a great many people.
In Terra Cotta Town.
I named roses wild flowers. (pp. 150–51)

Although a fixed identity is no longer possible, neither in the course of a dialogue nor in the words themselves, the intimate, personal atmosphere with
allusions to the female body observed above suggests female presences. We can
say that in spite of the indeterminacy of both words and characters, gender is
audible and visible: The female presence dominates.

Gender also plays an essential role with regard to the many names that are
mentioned in the play. The majority of these names are female, both first names
and surnames ("Mrs. Whitney," etc.). The pronoun "she," which appears frequently but does not have one single referent, equally creates a female circle of
characters. Thus, on the one hand, a fixed identity of the dramatic characters is
undermined, on the other hand, a female identity is suggested by the dominant
use of female names and pronouns.

Typical of Stein's general dramatic technique, *A Circular Play* undercuts coherent dramatic dialogue and the fixed identity of characters. Circles not only
emphasize the nonlinear movement of time within the play but also encompass
the speaker(s) and the reader or spectator without ever limiting his or her reception in either time or space. As is characteristic of postmodern theater, Stein's
play creates *moments* out of absence of coherence, linearity, and argumentation.
I am thinking particularly of Robert Wilson and Richard Foreman who are the
most prominent representatives of postmodern theater. Both try to break up time
by focusing on the moment and by ignoring any progressive action or plot.
Interestingly enough, both acknowledge that they are deeply influenced by
Stein. For Wilson, Stein's work always offers a lot of space for one's own
thoughts, as if one were in a landscape. This openness enables him, as he puts it,
to watch and listen simultaneously.[10] Comparing Richard Foreman's concept of
theater to Stein's plays, Kate Davy speaks of a "psychic" or "aesthetic distance"
that enables the spectator to resist identification or emotional involvement.[11]

The last line of the play does not end the "play in circles"; as is the case with
many works by Stein, the play ends with a question that not only leaves everything open but is self-reflective about the play and its circles: "I wonder if I have
heard about those circles" (p. 151). It is not clear whether "those" refers to the
two preceding lines "Fourteen circles" and "Fifteen circles" (p. 151), or to all of
the play's circles. Even circles that have no beginning or end are "open" enough
for the speaker who does not even trust the play's many forms and utterances of
and about circles. Stein's concept of the circle as a guideline for the play cannot
be taken for granted. Indeed, how could one trust a play with such a title?

And yet, the spatial metaphor of the circle fits Stein's "unstructured
structure"—a label that, according to Dinnah Pladott, can be applied to all of
Stein's operas and plays.[12]

The circle has neither an origin to which it can be traced back, nor does it allow a successive order; only repetition and circularity are possible. Circularity

and repetition as shaping "structures" of language must finally challenge the representational claim of language. If we believe that language can present something *as it is*, then we have to rely on a system of polarities in order to decide between what is (real) and what is represented (imitated), order/disorder, old/new, etc. In Chapter 4's analysis of Stein's play *Ladies' Voices* I will try to show how she invents a language that avoids reliance on such binary thinking and instead creates indeterminate relationships between words—and voices.

NOTES

1. "Dramatic text" and "performance text" are used by Keir Elam to differentiate between the text composed *for* the theater and the text produced *in* the theater. See *The Semiotics of Theatre and Drama* (London: Methuen, 1980), p. 2.

2. Gertrude Stein, *Lectures in America*, p. 93.

3. Gertrude Stein, *A Circular Play*, in *Last Operas and Plays*, ed. Carl Van Vechten (New York: Rinehart & Co., 1949), p. 139. Further page references appear in the text.

4. Renée Riese Hubert, "Gertrude Stein, Cubism, and the Postmodern Book," in *Postmodern Genres*, ed. Marjorie Perloff (Norman: University of Oklahoma Press, 1989), p. 105.

5. Although the speaker is not identified, I assume that it is a female speaker according to Susan Sniader Lanser. See my Chapter 1, note no. 11. I suggest that Lanser's observation is also pertinent to a dramatic text that has an unidentified first-person speaker and is written by a woman.

6. Betsy Alayne Ryan, *Gertrude Stein's Theatre of the Absolute* (Ann Arbor, MI: U.M.I. Research Press, 1980), p. 90.

7. Lisa Ruddick comments on these images in her "A Rosy Charm: Gertrude Stein and the Repressed Feminine," in Hoffman, *Critical Essays on Gertrude Stein* (Boston: G. K. Hall, 1986), p. 226.

8. Stein, *The Geographical History of America*, p. 77.

9. Hubert, "Gertrude Stein, Cubism, and the Postmodern Book," in *Postmodern Genres*, p. 106.

10. Robert Wilson in an interview with Peter Krumme and Gerhard Ahrens in the playbill for the performance of Stein's *Doctor Faustus Lights the Lights* (Berlin: Hebbel-Theater, 1992), p. 20.

11. Kate Davy, "Richard Foreman's Ontological-Hysteric Theatre: The Influence of Gertrude Stein," *Twentieth Century Review* 24, no. 1 (Spring 1978): 120.

12. Dinnah Pladott, "Gertrude Stein: Exile, Feminism, Avant-Garde in the American Theater," in *Modern American Drama: The Female Canon*, ed. June Schlueter (Rutherford, NJ: Fairleigh Dickinson University Press, 1990), p. 114.

4

The Multiple Voices of
Ladies' Voices (1916)

The title of this 50-line play is significant with regard to gender and genre: "Ladies' voices" includes the (linguistic) sign for the female and a potential communicative capability. "Lady," like "woman," can designate the female in general, but the term also raises expectations with regard to a social position that "woman" or "female" does not. The communicative dimension can be connected with the theater and the subtitle, *Curtain Raiser*, announces that ladies' voices are to be heard in a public realm. Moreover, as is stated in the first sentence, "[l]adies' voices give pleasure,"[1] one is indeed reminded of *jouissance* in the sense of Julia Kristeva, namely that women's "pleasure" is beyond the phallic realm because it can break the symbolic order. The "pleasure" that these ladies provide obviously derives from the fact that there is a dialogue; since they *talk together* ("Ladies voices together," p. 203), a close relationship is created that arouses pleasure for the women and for the reader/spectator/listener as well. Although there is no coherence in the course of the conversation, bits and pieces of familiar everyday conversations are recognizable. As Marie-Claire Pasquier points out, Stein, like Robert Wilson in many of his postmodern dramatic texts, relies on pieces of conversation but not on contexts.[2] Indeed, parts of the dialogue seem to have been "recorded" from snatches of conversations and then arranged according to Stein's compositional technique. Composition is central to her philosophy and literary aesthetics; as she explains in *Composition as Explanation*, she, writer and genius, says or writes what "everybody knows" and "everybody says."[3] Composing is therefore rearranging, and it is exactly the creative rearrangement of (common) conversations that is the underlying principle of *Ladies' Voices*.

Besides the everyday language of the ladies' voices, one must also consider the presence of the lesbian subject. In *Lifting Belly*, an explicit description of lesbian lovemaking, the word "Caesar" appears as it does in *Ladies' Voices*. "Caesar" is a typically "multivocal" Steinian word. In *Lifting Belly* it can even be the name of a speaker: "You have addressed me as Caesar" (*YGS*, p. 28). In the plural form it can designate breasts: "Lifting belly is so round. Big Caesars. Two Caesars. Little seize her" (*YGS*, p. 22), or "I say lifting belly gently and Caesars gently. . . . I say lifting belly and Caesars and cow come out" (*YGS*, p. 30).[4] Moreover, "Caesar" is a pun on "seize her" and "seizer," the one who grasps or acts.[5] The appearance of "Caesar" in *Ladies' Voices* is not explicitly linked with female sexuality because "Caesar" is referred to as a person: "Yes Genevieve does not know it. What. That we are seeing Caesar. Caesar kisses. Kisses today" (p. 203). Yet, given the meanings and importance of "Caesar" in Stein's work, the sexual realm needs to be considered here. In a conversation among ladies, the use of a term that implies lesbian lovemaking radically introduces a topic tabooed at the time Stein was writing. A lady is not expected to speak about such topics publicly; otherwise, she is not a lady.

The specific rearrangement of words and phrases creates a text that deconstructs the traditional play, first through the use of incoherent snatches of conversation, and second through the indirect presentation of the sexual relationships among the ladies. Stein does not help us to make connections between the single lines, nor does she develop a plot or a coherent conversation; the words she uses appear as colloquial phrases among women who know each other. Yet, this colloquial style can also be deciphered as a (lesbian) code, familiar to the women who use it and who do not have to rely on a common sequence of words in order to understand each other. The familiar words and casual phrases create intimacy and an atmosphere in which these female speakers (or voices) feel at ease and at home.

The linguistic code among these female speakers is not based on polarity, hierarchy, or (sexual) difference. Unlike the phallogocentric subject, the lesbian subject is not based on the subject/object distinction, which, as Lacan emphasizes, is based on a desire for what one is lacking; it is "as desire of the Other that man's desire finds form."[6] Instead, the lesbian subject engages in a relationship in which there is an interaction of a "lesbian Subject" and a "lesbian Other/self," terms used by Penelope Engelbrecht in an attempt to theorize the lesbian subject.[7] As Engelbrecht states, the term "lesbian" refers to both women and they can belong to either category. Although the relationship can be described in heterosexual terms, as Stein does (e.g., "husband," "wife"), the desire that structures their relationship is based on *mutual* desire. Contrary to the subject/object relationship, the lesbian subject desires the Other that is of the same.

Instead of polarity and dichotomy it is mutuality that determines the aesthetic principle of the conversation between the female speakers of *Ladies' Voices*. The kind of intimate "double-talk"[8] that characterizes Stein's dialogic language is multivocal and always comprises "an other" that is not polarized; part of the language used by these speakers is not final but always continuing. Gilbert and Gubar's phrase "language of love and love of language,"[9] though applied to *Lifting Belly*, also describes the er(r)otics of this language. The sentences "Did you say they were different. I said it made no difference. / Where does it. Yes." (p. 204) are indeterminate but demonstrate at the same time intimacy and acceptance between the speakers, although it is never clear to whom we have to attribute which parts of the conversation. Thus, the playful and er(r)otic indeterminacy of language is increased. *Ladies' Voices* is a play between *women*, but it is also a play between *words* uttered by female speakers. The generic label "play" is transformed and extended at the same time: it is verbal, erotic and generic play.

NOTES

1. Gertrude Stein, *Ladies' Voices*, in *Geography and Plays* (1922; reprint, New York: Haskell House, 1967), p. 203. Further page references appear in the text.

2. Marie-Claire Pasquier, "Gertrude Stein: un théâtre 'post-moderne'?" *Delta* 10 (May 1980): 51.

3. Gertrude Stein, *Composition as Explanation* (London: Hogarth Press, 1926); reprinted in *Selected Writings of Gertrude Stein*, ed. Carl Van Vechten (New York: Random House, 1962), p. 513.

4. Other passages in which "Caesar" or "Caesars" appear can be found in "A Sonatina Followed by Another," in *Bee Time Vine*, p. 26; or "The King or Something," in *Geography and Plays*, p. 127.

5. See also Penelope J. Engelbrecht's comment on "Caesar," in "'Lifting Belly Is a Language': The Postmodern Lesbian Subject," *Feminist Studies* 16, no. 1 (Spring 1990): 98. Engelbrecht points out that "Caesar" implies "that each lesbian is herself a 'Caesar,' a bedroom emperor, perhaps, or a 'seizer' (an actor) or even a source of nourishment (a 'breast')."

6. Jacques Lacan, *Ecrits: A Selection*, trans. Alan Sheridan (New York: Norton, 1977), p. 311.

7. Engelbrecht, "'Lifting Belly Is a Language,'" 88. In her most recent book, Teresa de Lauretis speaks of the lesbian subject as a "double one" because there are always *two* women to make a lesbian relationship. See *The Practice of Love: Lesbian Sexuality and Perverse Desire* (Bloomington: Indiana University Press, 1994).

8. Neil Schmitz, *Of Huck and Alice: Humorous Writing in American Literature* (Minneapolis: University of Minnesota Press, 1983), p. 185.

9. Sandra Gilbert and Susan Gubar, *No Man's Land: The Place of the Woman Writer in the Twentieth Century*, vol. 2 (New Haven, CT: Yale University Press, 1989), p. 244.

5

"Preparing for Opera": Gertrude Stein and Susan B. Anthony: Mothers of Us All

WHAT'S IN A NAME? IDENTITY, VOICE, AND VOTE

The "opera" *The Mother of Us All* is Stein's last longer work and one of the few with an explicitly feminist voice, although, unlike the protagonist Susan B. Anthony, Stein never actively participated in the women's suffrage movement. Anthony (1820–1906) was one of the leading American suffragists. We do not know why Stein chose this particular historical female figure, but she was obviously deeply interested in Anthony and her cause, since she conducted extensive research on Anthony and her period.[1] Stein's approach to this historical figure is similar to that in *Four in America*: She uses some of the historical material but also introduces entirely fictive elements; historical and fictive characters intermingle and enter into a dialogue with each other. Stein uses excerpts from Anthony's writings and incorporates them into her own text.[2] The boundary between the real, that is, historical, and the fictive is blurred: "there is no a priori 'reality' except the simulated reality or the simulacrum of reality that Stein conjures up on her madcap stage, where the 'real' and the fabricated have equal status."[3] In the chapters on the autobiographies I will point out that there is a constant shifting between the "discourse of art" and "the discourse of history"; here we have an even more radical blurring because on the one hand the immediacy of the theater world enhances the "reality" of the "real" events; on the other hand we watch a fictional character like Joe the Loiterer talk to historical personage Susan B. Anthony. The two realms of the "real" and fictive events are no longer distinguishable; opposites do not exist in Stein's literary creativity.

A further example of Stein's questioning and challenging of rules, hierarchies, and categories is her use of the opera genre. As in Stein's plays, we are confronted with descriptions of objects and persons and not with a plot. These descriptions are not structured according to a temporal or spatial order.

Past and present merge; here and now change constantly, and a sort of timelessness is created. There is no cathartic moment as found traditionally in operas (or plays),[4] and Stein's opera does not end climactically.

Disregarding rules and generic conventions, Stein creates her own Susan B. Anthony by giving her a voice—but not yet a vote—through deconstructing the voices of her male opponents. Right at the beginning, the unusual prologue—it is sung by the figure of Virgil Thomson, the composer of the opera's music who is not an opponent of Anthony—challenges notions of power, justice, and wealth. Virgil T., as he is named, sings about a persecutor who will himself be persecuted one day. These introductory lines already express—in the typical Steinian wordplay—the potential reversal of power relations, and introduce the topic of the struggle for political and economic equality. It is not quite clear who represents the persecutor; *he* may be associated with Daniel Webster (1782–1852), patriarchal statesman and Anthony's main (fictional) antagonist. The ambiguity inherent in the designations of persecutor and persecuted emphasizes the problematics of power structures under which especially women and African Americans[5] in the nineteenth century had to suffer. After this prologue, Virgil T. sits down and sings the following text: "Begin to sit. / Begins to sit. / He begins to sit. / That's why. / Begins to sit. / And that is the reason why."[6] The illogical repetitions and the variations of the sentence "Begins to sit" linguistically depict the sometimes empty words of those who *sit* on the bench and are judges over right or wrong, just or unjust. After these introductory lines about the problematic attributions of right and wrong, the first act begins.

Stein's investigation of dichotomies such as right/wrong, true/false, rich/poor, old/new, and, above all, male/female occurs in various realms in this opera. The most obvious realm concerns language, as in the prologue. At the beginning of the first act Stein relies on one of the proverbs from the Old Testament[7] to explore rightful authority. Significantly, Daniel Webster speaks these opening words: "He digged a pit, he digged it deep he digged it for his brother. / Into the pit he did fall in the pit he digged for tother" (p. 53). This proverb, used by a statesman and an orator, exemplifies patriarchal (biblical) authority for morally correct behavior, but it also questions male aggressive attitudes toward another male opponent.

The reference to patriarchal tradition continues as "all the Characters" proclaim that their fathers were called Daniel, and a character called G. S. speaks about her father, "bearded Daniel" (p. 53). Gertrude Stein's father was named Daniel, and so was Susan B. Anthony's. Patriarchal tradition and names are intricately connected as Anthony makes clear at her first appearance in the opera: "Susan B. Anthony is my name to choose a name is feeble" (p. 53). She addresses another woman, Indiana Elliot, who is about to get married and is willing to change, that is, to choose, her name. "What's in a name," Indiana Elliot asks, and Anthony's response "Everything" (p. 53) points to the importance of names and naming and their social and political implications. For Anthony name and identity belong together; she considers marriage to be an impossible option because this social contract demands the fusion of two, wife and husband, which contradicts Anthony's concept of "one all one":

I am not married and the reason why is that I have had to do what I have had to do, I have had to be what I have had to be, I could never be one of two I could never be two in one as married couples do and can, I am but one all one, one and all one, and so I have never been married to any one. (p. 75)

Anthony's description of "one" actually implies more than one "one": the grammatical unit "one all one" is slightly reminiscent of Stein's "I am I," which also creates a symmetrical relationship between the two pronouns. "One" and "I" are not positioned alone and thus refer to the necessity of dialogue without losing independence and autonomy. Anthony's concept of this dynamic, independent self is in sharp contrast to the view of marriage dominant at the time of the historical figure Anthony. In an 1895 interview she describes how a married woman loses autonomy and identity:

In fact, I never felt I could give up my life of freedom to become a man's housekeeper. When I was young, if a girl married poor, she became a housekeeper and a drudge. If she married wealth she became a pet and a doll. Just think, had I married at twenty, I would have been a drudge or a doll for fifty-five years. Think of it![8]

Stein's Anthony similarly fights against the social and economic restrictions faced by a married woman. This struggle for equal rights and for women's vote and voice is so absorbing that her own voice tends to remain separate despite the above-mentioned desire for dialogism; Anthony's voice is a solitary one among those of the other characters.[9] This single position is also pertinent to the historical Anthony, who was ridiculed, accused, and even sentenced because she voted. She did not live to see her goal achieved (only fourteen years after her death were women allowed to vote). Stein as writer and artist was similarly belittled and never really acknowledged during her lifetime except by very few people and critics, although she was in a constant dialogue with others—above all with Toklas. *The Mother of Us All,* written shortly before her death, is a powerful and moving presentation of the loneliness of a woman fighting for her rights.

The links between names, selfhood, and patriarchal and matriarchal traditions are further explored in other characters of the opera. Indiana Elliot not only asks the crucial question "What's in a name"; her name also contains important references to other names, namely those of women writers. Elliot, the most obvious sign, alludes to Stein's favorite author George Eliot, whose name Stein sometimes spelt "Elliot."[10] Like Indiana Elliot, George Eliot chose a name, although, as we know, for other reasons. But the allusion to George Eliot the writer is especially pertinent in the context of *The Mother of Us All* because it manifests another of Stein's literary foremothers. Indeed, the name Indiana Elliot contains references to two other literary foremothers: Charlotte Brontë, whose Jane Eyre uses the name "Elliott" in order not to disclose her identity, and George Sand, who published a novel called *Indiana.*[11] Moreover, both writers, like George Eliot, used pseudonyms. Indeed, there is "everything" in a name, as Anthony has proclaimed, and Stein's web of different allusions makes us aware that names are social constructions like identity, and not fixed entities. The various allusions to literary foremothers emphasize the importance of women writers on the one hand, but they also point to the obstacles that they have to overcome in a patriarchal society and that have necessitated the choices of masculine pseudonyms. Constance Fletcher is another female character in the opera who wrote under a pseudonym in real life; she is known as the author George Fleming and was a friend of Stein's.[12]

The female tradition evoked through these characters has a male counterpart in the patriarchal figure of Daniel Webster. He not only is Anthony's antagonist but also represents a paternalistic, thoughtless, and reckless attitude directed mostly toward women, African Americans, and the poor. He is incapable of having a dialogue because disagreeing seems to be his principle, as is shown at the very beginning of his political debate with Anthony:

Susan B.	I hear a sound.
Jo the Loiterer.	Yes well
Daniel Webster.	I do not hear a sound. When I am told.
Susan B.	Silence.
	(Everybody is silent) (p. 57)

Webster not only ignores other people's voices but also falls asleep during a speech delivered by Anthony. Without regret he frankly admits his disgraceful behavior: "I did sleep on the gentleman's speech; and slept soundly" (p. 58). Although he refers to Anthony's speech, he uses the male pronoun; indeed, he always uses male pronouns when mentioning her. This male linguistic arrogance enhances Webster's ineptness toward a woman with a voice of her own.[13] Such discriminatory acts contribute to the solitude of Anthony's voice.

Webster belongs to the group ironically called "The Three V.I.P.'s," which includes Andrew Johnson (1808–1875; 17th president of the United States) and Thaddeus Stevens (1792–1868; American politician); these three Americans represent patriarchal and patriotic tradition. Furthermore, the three men exhibit a self-centeredness that is mirrored in their repetitive and univocal (chorus) use of language. The following conversation between the three V.I.P.'s and Anthony illustrates this difference in self-awareness; the three men's words are only uttered to be received by others without considering the recipients:

> We are the chorus of the V.I.P.
> Very important persons to every one who can hear and see, we are the chorus of the V.I.P.

| Susan B. | Yes, so they are. I am important but not that way, not that way. |

The Three V.I.P.'s   We you see we V.I.P. very important to any one who can hear
                          or you can see, just we three, of course lots of others but just
                          we three, just we three we are the chorus of V.I.P. (p. 68)

After the first debate between Anthony and Webster, a so-called interlude
takes place between Anthony and her friend Anne (who does not have a second
name in the opera), which differs sharply from the conversation between Anthony and Webster: Anthony and Anne engage in a genuine dialogue, listening
to each other's arguments. Interestingly enough, the interlude itself is given another generic label: "(Susan B. A Short Story)" (p. 59). This "short story" in
prose with two speakers undermines the dramatic form of the opera on the one
hand, and also questions the genre "short story" because its dominant form is
the dialogue. The interlude begins with a short piece that is also typographically
marked as a dramatic form:

> Yes I was said Susan.
> You mean you are, said Anne.
> No said Susan no.
> When this you see remember me said Susan B.
> I do said Anne. (p. 59)[14]

The short piece illustrates both the intimacy between the two women and
Anne's encouraging, affirmative attitude toward Anthony. While Webster only
uses rhetorical phrases, bits and pieces of patriotic speeches, or does not listen at
all, Anne listens carefully and tries to understand her friend's position. The dialogue between Anthony and Anne not only creates intimacy between the two
women but also provides evidence for the positive effect of contradicting
positions in a dialogue. In spite of Anne's affirmative function, she also
contradicts her friend and urges her to leave her home again and to speak to the
people for the cause. The domestic sphere in which this conversation takes place
incorporates the political realm. Other scenes in which the two women are also
at home and discussing political matters are introduced as "Susan B. doing her
house-work in her house" (p. 76) or "Susan B. Anthony busy with her
housework" [sic] (p. 79). This mixing of the private with the public is more
pertinent to women's lives, while their strict separation is usually typical in the
life of a man: The three V.I.P.'s are never shown washing dishes.

  The dramatic form of the conversation is broken up again and again by a
third-person narrator, but without interrupting the flow of words between the
two women. The following passage illustrates how the speakers' first-person
pronoun "I" and the presence and mediation of a narrator are complementary:

Anne was reproachful why do you not speak louder she said to Susan B. I speak as
loudly as I can said Susan B. I even speak louder I even speak louder than I can. Do you
really said Anne. Yes I really do said Susan B. it was dark and as it was dark it was
necessary to speak louder or very softly, very softly. Dear me said Susan B., if it was not
so early I would be sleepy. I myself said Anne never like to look at a newspaper. You are
entirely right said Susan B. only I disagree with you. You do said Anne. You know very
well I do said Susan B. (p. 60)

Although the narrator is mainly noticeable through the dominant tags "said
Susan B." or "said Anne," the conversation has an additional voice that inten-
sifies the dialogic element; naming the two women contributes to the necessary
distinction of two autonomous voices. This prose interlude cannot be defined
generically, yet it is not a "genreless" text because the "interlude" and the "short
story" are mixed in the sense Derrida uses the word ("gattieren"). Indeed,
Stein's manuscripts of the opera also point to this mixing of texts: Among the
original manuscripts of *The Mother of Us All* (1945), there is a separate
notebook called "Susan B. Anthony. A Short Story." In another manuscript
(1945–1946) with the title *The Mother of Us All, an Opera in Two Acts and
Interlude*, the interlude is missing, but there is a note saying "The short story."
As I have already mentioned with regard to the composition of *Ida A Novel*,
Stein's method of composing is more a piecing together than a progressive
uniform writing practice. Single texts written at different times can become parts
of a whole without being submitted to generic classification. Similar to
Anthony's "mixing" of the private with the political, the interlude and the short
story are generic forms for both realms and are not separated.

IS THE RIGHT (TO) VOTE THE MALE VOTE?

At the end of Stein's opera women have the right to vote. But significantly,
Susan B. Anthony's voice is only heard from behind a statue: She has the vote
and voice, but her body is absent. The ambiguity inherent in this disembodiment
with regard to her achievement is increased by her last words:

> Where is where. In my long life of effort and strife, dear life, life is strive, in my long
> life, it will not come and go, I tell you so, it will stay it will pay but
>   (A long silence)
> But do I want what we have got, has it not gone, what made it live, has it not gone
> because now it is had, in my long life in my long life
>   (Silence)
> Life is strife, I was a martyr all my life not to what I won but to what was done.
>   (Silence)
> Do you know because I tell you so, or do you know, do you know.
>   (Silence)
> My long life, my long life. (pp. 87–88)

Anthony's voice behind the statue no longer expresses protest against male
oppression, but it does not convey satisfaction either. Doubts about the significance of women's vote overshadow her success. Her question "But do I want
what we have got" points to the problematic equality between women and men:
Women's right to vote depends on a male right and tradition, and therefore
women might become like men. Earlier in the opera Anthony had voiced a mistrust of the risks of equal positions: "having the vote they will become like men,
they will be afraid, having the vote will make them afraid" (p. 81). Men are
afraid, as Anthony explains, because "they are afraid of black men" and of
women (p. 80); thus, women practicing a patriarchal right run the risk of

adapting to patriarchal authority in general, and thus would lose their potential for protest, contradiction, and dialogue.[15] Anthony's probing question about her achievement remains unanswered; the opera ends with her question "do you know," inviting us to express our own answers with our voices.

Anthony's disillusionment and her solitude—contrary to the historical Anthony[16]—reminds us of Stein's own singular position as an unacknowledged artist during her lifetime.

Anthony as "the mother of us all" in Stein's text fights for her daughters' voices because she believes in the power of the word; to voice one's desire is life-giving. It is the mother who first speaks or sings to her children. This impact of the maternal voice is emphasized in Hélène Cixous' "The Laugh of the Medusa":

In women's speech, as in their writing, that element which never stops resonating, which, once we've been permeated by it, profoundly and imperceptibly touched by it, retains the power of moving us—that element is the song: first music from the first voice of love which is alive in every woman. Why this privileged relationship with the voice? Because no woman stockpiles as many defenses for countering the drives as does a man. You don't build walls around yourself, you don't forego pleasure as "wisely" as he. Even if phallic mystification has generally contaminated good relationships, a woman is never far from "mother" (I mean outside her role functions: the "mother" as nonname and as source of goods).[17]

Stein's Anthony, "the mother of us all," represents this first voice that can empower other women. The significance of Anthony's maternal position can also be linked with Julia Kristeva's concept of the presymbolic, or the semiotic which is essential in the pre-Oedipal mother-child relationship. Their communication is mainly determined by rhythm, gesture, and melody. Although these characteristics are much more dominant in other, more experimental works by Stein, Anthony's language represents a kind of mother tongue because she speaks a language that contrasts and challenges the patriarchal discourse used by her male antagonists, and that serves other women. Male discourse is presented as non-communicative and monologic. As it is contrasted with Susan B. Anthony's it is depreciated and deconstructed because Anthony's discourse is the one enabling women to get the vote.

The deconstruction of male discourse goes hand in hand with the deconstruction of the genre opera: There is neither a plot nor a recognizable temporal or spatial pattern of the scenes or acts. Neither time nor space are determined by the patriarchal fathers of the nation (e.g., Daniel Webster with the association to Stein's and Anthony's fathers) because Stein manipulates centuries (she plays with chronology). Anthony's voice permeates both the temporal and spatial realms, and opens them for other women. Her open question, "do you know," at the end of the opera undermines any ending, and the periods of silence enhance the indeterminacy. Paradoxically, silence and voice both belong to Anthony's language.[18] Moreover, the voice is separated from the real body, which is replaced by a statue. This disconnection attributes more weight to language than

to the bodily presence of its creatress, Anthony—and Stein. It is not coincidental
that at the end of her life Stein wrote a text about a figure who, like herself,
fought against the patriarchal law of the word. Being autobiographical in many
respects, this opera has a historical figure as its protagonist; in the next chapter I
will explore why the protagonist of Stein's autobiographies is not merely Stein
herself.

NOTES

1. See James R. Mellow, *Charmed Circle* (New York: Praeger, 1974) p. 463. In a
letter to Carl Van Vechten, Stein mentions a biography she read, namely *Susan B.
Anthony: The Woman Who Changed the Mind of a Nation* (New York: Frederick A
Stokes Co., 1928). See *The Letters of Gertrude Stein and Carl Van Vechten 1913–1946*,
ed. Edward Burns (New York: Columbia University Press, 1986), vol. 2, p. 798.

2. For more information on the use of historical material, see Elizabeth Winston,
"Making History in *The Mother of Us All*," *Mosaic: Journal for the Interdisciplinary
Study of Literature* 20, no. 4 (Fall 1987): 122–25.

3. Dinnah Pladott, "Gertrude Stein: Exile, Feminism, Avant-Garde in the American
Theater," in *Modern American Drama: The Female Canon*, ed. June Schlueter
(Rutherford, NJ: Fairleigh Dickinson University Press, 1990), p. 121.

4. For a definition of opera, see Herbert Lindenberger, who ascribes to the opera an
elaborate, heroic style: "As an art-form intimately connected with the reigning
establishment, it is no wonder that opera projects an image of something considerably
larger than life," "From Opera to Postmodernity: On Genre, Style, Institutions," in
Postmodern Genres, ed. Marjorie Perloff (Norman: University of Oklahoma Press,
1989), pp. 28–29.

5. Like many other suffragists Susan B. Anthony also fought for the vote for African
Americans.

6. Gertrude Stein, *The Mother of Us All*, in *Last Operas and Plays*, ed. Carl Van
Vechten (New York: Rinehart, 1949), p. 52. All references in the text are from this
edition.

7. Proverbs 26:27.

8. Nelly Bly interview, in *Woman's Journal*, February 22, 1895. Quoted in Kathleen
Barry, *Susan B. Anthony: A Biography of a Singular Feminist* (New York: New York
University Press, 1988), p. 231.

9. Harriet Chessman even speaks of an "isolated 'I'" with regard to Anthony, in
Chessman, *The Public Is Invited to Dance: Representation, the Body, and Dialogue in
Gertrude Stein* (Stanford, CA: Stanford University Press 1989), p. 200.

10. For example, in the notebooks for *The Making of Americans*, Box I, D: "Alice's
resemblance to George Elliot interesting" (Beinecke Rare Book and Manuscript Library,
Yale University).

11. For more detailed information on the allusions to these literary foremothers, see
Elizabeth Winston, "Making History in *The Mother of Us All*": 120–22. I gratefully
acknowledge her information on George Sand's novel *Indiana*.

12. Fletcher wrote the story "By Accident," which is now again available in Elaine
Showalter's recent anthology *Daughters of Decadence: Women Writers of the Fin-de-
Siècle* (London: Virago, 1993), pp. 74–83. Significantly, it is a story about a married
woman's unhappiness.

13. Robert K. Martin explains that the use of the male pronoun is "mere convention of parliamentary speech," but he also points out that Webster's attitude here excludes women from speech. See "*The Mother of Us All* and American History," in *Gertrude Stein and the Making of Literature*, ed. Neuman and Nadel, p. 217.

14. The sentence "When this you see remember me" is a quotation from *Little Lord Fauntleroy* by Frances Hodgson Burnett (London: Penguin Puffin, 1981). Fauntleroy gives Mr. Hobbs a case in which is written "When this you see, remember me" (p. 43). It expresses Lord Fauntleroy's wish not to be forgotten by his friend. Anthony's use of this well-known phrase may allude to her fear of not being heard, of being forgotten. I thank Hartwig Isernhagen for this reference to Burnett. It seems that this line was quite meaningful for Stein because it turns up again and again in her texts—for example, at the very end of *Four Saints in Three Acts*, when one of the saints uses this phrase. *Last Operas and Plays*, p. 480.

15. Chessman comments on the danger that women's vote implies: "To make the vote literal, to materialize it and so to make it vulnerable to ownership, is paradoxically to allow its participation in a system of representation whereby what is signified becomes absent, its place usurped by the sign itself" (Chessman, *The Public Is Invited to Dance*, p. 201).

16. See also Elizabeth Winston, "Making History in *The Mother of Us All*," p.125; or Jane Palatini Bowers, *"They Watch Me as They Watch This": Gertrude Stein's Metadrama*, p. 125.

17. Hélène Cixous, "The Laugh of the Medusa," in *New French Feminisms*, p. 251.

18. My thanks to Katherine Henry for her helpful comment on the frequent periods of silence in this final passage. Henry states that in the course of Anthony's final speech her words become less and less specific and enter the private realm of silence."What's in a Name: Law, Language, and Identity in *The Mother of Us All*," unpublished seminar paper (English Department, Rutgers University, 1991).

III

Auto-Bio-Graphies

6

Whose Autobiography? I/Eye and Everybody's Autobiographies

As already illustrated, Gertrude Stein will often use a generic label only to produce a work that does not conform to the main characteristics one would expect of a particular genre. This incongruity can also be found in her autobiographies. Works with explicit titles such as *The Autobiography of Alice B. Toklas* or *Everybody's Autobiography* cannot be taken as genuine autobiographies because their generic classification can be debated, and because there are other works by Stein that are also autobiographies. The definition of this genre with regard to Stein's texts is further complicated in that Stein's critics subsume different works under the autobiography genre.

Feminist genre theory has recently contributed a great deal to the revived discussion about the criteria of autobiography. One of the important issues in this discussion concerns the position of the female autobiographer and aspects of (her) subjectivity. Observations about the female subject and its representations have shown that there is a tendency in women's writing to blur genres or to use various discourses, among them, frequently, the autobiographical mode. As a consequence the so-called traditional criteria for one specific genre can no longer be applied; they have to be questioned and tested, especially with regard to gender. Moreover, as autobiography seems to be a genre often used by women writers, we have to explore the reasons for this preference.

Although deconstructionist theory has claimed that we must do away with notions of a centered self that is not shattered, split, or destabilized, we must seriously ask ourselves whether and in how far this can be applied to the female self, which has never been considered to be whole at all. How then can it become shattered? And we must pay heed to the warning given by Sidonie Smith:

Already elided, woman now confronts the impossibility of ever finding a space through which to insert/assert her own agency. Thus while we celebrate certain ramifications of the breakdown of metaphysical selfhood—certainly its undermining of the authority of the father in one of his guises—we cannot go so far down the path of postmodernism that we accept our total subjection in discursive regimes.[1]

Thus, keeping this warning in mind, we should be attentive to the silenced voices of marginalized speakers while making use of the destabilization of the old self. Unusual and multiple discursive forms of self-representation by marginalized writers can become possible and be perceived as such without being stigmatized or ignored. Clear characteristics of a self-narrative can no longer be applied; therefore, the notion of a single, unified self cannot be expected, but at the same time, notions of the fragmented self without taking gender into consideration must be questioned. Therefore, female self-representation may appear in forms that fit neither definition.

Stein's preoccupation with autobiography raises questions about the self and ways of writing about it, which provide evidence for her "postmodern" insight. Stein's approach is postmodern in the sense that she questions a stable self and realizes that the dynamic of writing does not create one "right" meaning. Thus, multiple sites of the self are possible:

And identity is funny being yourself is funny as you are never yourself to yourself except as you remember yourself and then of course you do not believe yourself. That is really the trouble with an autobiography you do not of course you do not really believe yourself why should you, you know so well so very well that it is not yourself, it could not be yourself because you cannot remember right and if you do remember right it does not sound right and of course it does not sound right because it is not right. You are of course never yourself.[2]

Stein describes the crucial problem of a person trying to write down his or her autobiography: It is the act of remembering that already establishes a distance between (your)self of the very moment and of the self of the past. This difference in time seems to be the reason why "it does not sound right" and "is not right." Stein addresses a similar problem when she explains her uneasiness about plays (cf. Chapter 3 on the plays); plays should not refer back to the past but concentrate on the moment. "[T]he composition of the present time" (*LA*, p. 104) is her artistic goal, be it in a play or an autobiography. If one insists on the present, writing one's autobiography indeed becomes a problem. Therefore, "you are never yourself to yourself" because the moment you write down your perceptions of yourself you are more than the (one) self you were a moment ago.

A reading of Stein's autobiographies will show that her attempt to write autobiography led her to experiment with and subvert traditional autobiography. One consequence of this subversion is the above-mentioned difficulty in deciding which works we can subsume under the autobiography genre. In *Stanzas in Meditation*, written at the same time as *The Autobiography of Alice B. Toklas*, the speaker states: "This is her [Alice's] autobiography one of two / But which it is no one which it is can know";[3] numerous other passages show that Stein's poetic "meditations" describe the relationship between her and Alice B. Toklas

around 1935.[4] While *Stanzas in Meditation* is a work generally regarded as poetry, *Everybody's Autobiography* is written in a prose form that is able to
incorporate many theoretical statements about writing, and *How to Write*, a very
hermetic and difficult work, alludes to many personal events in Stein's life.
Wars I Have Seen (1942–1944), Stein's memoirs of World War II, begins like a
conventional autobiography, namely with the phrase "I was born," but because
of its focus on the war, it is rarely considered an autobiography. Many critics
regard it as a personal description of World War II experiences.[5] *Paris France*
(1939) is another work written in the autobiographical mode, but as its title suggests, France and the French character are the dominant themes in this short
book about Stein's childhood memories of Paris and her observations about
daily French life as an adult.

Both *Wars I Have Seen* and *Paris France* present rich material for ethnographic analysis. Stein describes her life in France with a mind that is responsive
to the little necessities of daily life as well as to crucial cultural (national) movements. *Wars I Have Seen* is a documentary of what it meant to live in occupied
France during World War II and to cope with the difficulties of providing food
or wood every day.

All of the works mentioned above share one essential characteristic: They are
thematically concerned with identity and self. But as the self is never the *one*
you describe because of time that comes between the self and "the composition
of the present time," Stein's autobiographies, or works that deal with the self,
never contain one voice only, that is, the speaking voice of the author. I have
chosen *The Autobiography of Alice B. Toklas*, *Everybody's Autobiography*, and
Wars I Have Seen as autobiographies that focus on the presentation of the self. I
will not discuss *Paris France* because it deals more with cultural and aesthetic
aspects than with questions of the self. *The Geographical History of America*, a
book that explores the human mind and human nature, is about the self also, but
as it describes less of Stein's life than the three other works, it will not be discussed here.

NOTES

1. Sidonie Smith, "Self, Subject, and Resistance: Marginalities and Twentieth-
Century Autobiographical Practice," *Tulsa Studies in Women's Literature* 9, no. 1
(Spring 1990): 14.

2. Gertrude Stein, *Everybody's Autobiography* (New York: Random House, 1937), p.
68.

3. Gertrude Stein, *Stanzas in Meditation and Other Poems (1929–1933)*, vol. 6 of the
Yale Edition of the Unpublished Writings of Gertrude Stein (New Haven, CT: Yale
University Press, 1956; reprint, Freeport, NY: Books for Libraries Press, 1969), p. 77.

4. See Ulla E. Dydo, "*Stanzas in Meditation*: The Other Autobiography," *Chicago
Review* 35, no. 2 (Winter 1985): 4–20.

5. See for example, Monika Hoffmann, *Gertrude Steins Autobiographien: The
Autobiography of Alice B. Toklas und Everybody's Autobiography* (Frankfurt am Main:
Peter Lang, 1992), p. 97.

7

The Double-Voiced Autobiography

The Autobiography of Alice B. Toklas is one of the more accessible books by Stein, and it is not surprising that it is the book that brought Stein fame—and money. It was indeed written for the public, a public that approved of an "accepted lesbian life,"[1] because it is presented as a heterosexual arrangement. A heterosexual audience that does not know about Stein and Toklas's relationship would not necessarily recognize the two women as lesbians. The autobiography uses the voice of Alice B. Toklas to depict Gertrude Stein as a genius; it is not Stein herself who presents herself as a genius, but it is done by her lover and companion. Stein's strategy of speaking in her lover's voice enables her to ignore traditional patterns of autobiographies and yet create "a portrait of the (female) artist" whose authority is unquestioned because she is not recognizable as a sexual transgressor. Stein's self appears to be stable and not marginalized; indeed, disclosing so little about her inner life and her love relationship with Toklas, but so much more about all the celebrities that visited Stein and Toklas's home, it is not surprising that Stein could evade the threat of a marginalized self. The voice of Toklas becomes Stein's at the very end of the book:

About six weeks ago Gertrude Stein said, it does not look to me as if you were ever going to write that autobiography [Alice Toklas's]. You know what I am going to do. I am going to write it for you. I am going to write it as simply as Defoe did the autobiography of Robinson Crusoe. And she has and this is it.[2]

These last lines of the autobiography illustrate the difficulty of distinguishing between Stein as real author and character, and between Toklas as fictive author and character. The two "I"s of the real and fictive author merge. In the very last sentence, "And she [Stein] has and this is it," Toklas as the fictive author speaks again, but paradoxically and simultaneously denies being this author. Stein's dictum "I am II" becomes quite intelligible: Stein's self is never one, but always an "I" plus an "I"; "II" can be read as the Roman numeral two, or 1 plus 1 equals two, and so on.[3] Writing one's own self is not possible for Stein because her self is always in dialogue with another "I," and sometimes the other "I" is Toklas, but it can also be the reader or everybody.

Stein's reference to Defoe's "autobiography" of Robinson Crusoe at the end of *The Autobiography of Alice B. Toklas* contains a further key to her understanding of the self and its (self-)representation. The reference to Defoe can be read together with a passage from *Narration* (1935), in which Stein identifies the fictional character Crusoe with Defoe:

Think of Defoe, he tried to write Robinson Crusoe as if it were exactly what did happen and yet after all he is Robinson Crusoe and Robinson Crusoe is Defoe and therefore after all it is not what is happening it is what is happening to him to Robinson Crusoe that makes what is exciting every one.[4]

Stein tries to understand the relation between the autobiographer and the autobiography, that is, his or her creation of a self. Stein emphasizes that there is no difference between the two, and yet, the autobiographer's creation cannot describe what really happened because the autobiographer is never the same that he or she describes. Robinson Crusoe in the end is "what is exciting every one," and not Daniel Defoe. Moreover, the allusion to Robinson Crusoe's "autobiography" seems to imply that Defoe as the writer of the fictive *Robinson Crusoe* wrote his autobiography through this book. Thus, we might conclude, according to Stein, that a writer's creation of a person is always autobiographical.

Defoe and Crusoe as a pair in Stein's explanation can be compared to Stein and Toklas, although the latter were two real persons. Yet, the fact that Stein sees Crusoe as the one to whom "it is happening" suggests that the autobiographer's focus on a self other than his or her own is possible, whereas a focus on his or her own is not, for the above-mentioned reasons. The crucial implication of the Defoe/Crusoe passage in *Narration* is the dialogic element necessary between the writer and this other self. In Stein's case it is Toklas who is not only her "other" self in their love relationship but both listener and fictive narrator of Stein's self. Therefore, the title *The Autobiography of Alice B. Toklas* is not merely a hoax as some readers have taken it to be; it indicates the "subversive intent" of Stein's autobiography, which, in the end, cannot be one, because for Stein there is never one "I" but two, or even more: An I is an I is an I is an I.

The Defoe passage functions as a further link to Stein's "subversive intent" of *The Autobiography*: The realistic, though fictional details in *Robinson Crusoe* are to be taken as factual truth, a characteristic for which the book has become famous. Stein, though supposedly relying on Defoe's narrative strategy, presents fact as fiction, but also fiction as fact. This constant shifting, as Linda Hutcheon would say, between "the discourse of art" and "the discourse of history,"[5] points toward a multiplicity of positions that the self occupies. Furthermore, the "I" of one self can become the "eye" of the other self, watching or looking at the former without the appropriation of the male gaze, projecting its fantasy on this

this other, female self. I use "male gaze" here as it is used by film theoreticians such as Laura Mulvey.[6] Here, the female gaze, as it were, is used by both selves, both women.

This implied pun on "I"/"eye" emphasizes the importance of seeing, one of the three capabilities Stein relies on in her writing besides listening and talking. The first edition of the book demonstrates that looking is essential for this autobiography and for the identity of its author. In this first edition there are sixteen photographs carefully placed throughout the book[7] with a table of illustrations at the beginning. The first photograph on the frontispiece shows Stein at a table, writing, while Toklas, in the background, is standing at the door. The caption to this illustration gives the following information: "Alice B. Toklas at the door, photograph by Man Ray." Although Stein's name is not mentioned in writing, Stein is identified as (the) writer. As P. Adams Sitney aptly points out, the conversation between Stein and Toklas at the end of the book (quoted above) could be read "as an extended caption."[8] A reader opening the book will *look at* the photograph and see immediately that it is *not* Toklas who is the writer in the picture. The last photograph shows the first page of the manuscript, another link to the writer Stein sitting and writing at her desk in the first photograph. These signs referring to the identity of the actual autobiographer can be *seen*. Seeing one's self seems to be more accurate than writing one's self because seeing is concentrated on the present moment and can be caught immediately by the camera—and by the eye—whereas with writing—and reading—time and memory are involved.

Furthermore, the photograph on the frontispiece showing Stein and Toklas together in their home provides evidence of a close and intimate companionship. Both women are necessary for the creation of the "autobiography" whose focus is no longer on *one* self only.[9] Moreover, through Toklas as fictive autobiographer Stein can describe herself as a genius without seeming self-centered or arrogant. And Stein is not the exclusive center of the book's attention; Stein pays homage to her companion by giving her book this particular title. Thus, a reciprocal relationship is involved, which is both representative of their union in real life and of the double-voiced narrative strategy of this autobiography.

The first chapter of the book, dealing with Alice B. Toklas's life before she arrived in Paris ("Before I Came to Paris"), is barely three pages long, while the analogous chapter about Gertrude Stein's life before her arrival in Paris (Chapter 4, "Gertrude Stein Before She Came to Paris") runs about sixteen pages. This unevenness already indicates that the fictive autobiographer "knows" more about Stein's early years than about her own. Toklas's description of her early years ends when she meets Stein. But the sentence concluding this first chapter is pertinent to both women: "In this way my new full life began" (p. 5). Stein speaking for Toklas through Toklas's voice obviously also speaks for herself. The self, that is, the "auto" of the autobiography, is neither Stein's nor Toklas's alone but two female selves intermingling.

Toklas as narrator focuses on Stein as genius from the very beginning. She is the one who recognizes geniuses, and thus her judgment is given enormous weight: "I have only known three first class geniuses and in each case on sight within me something rang. In no one of the three cases [Gertrude Stein, Pablo Picasso and Alfred Whitehead] have I been mistaken" (p. 5). Although Stein makes Toklas present her as a genius, Toklas herself is also given a very special status as she is capable of knowing whether a person is a genius or not. Picasso and Whitehead, the two other geniuses, were already acknowledged celebrities in their field in 1933, which makes Toklas's statement even more pertinent. Grouping Stein with these two *male* geniuses is a clever strategy for two reasons: Stein was not a published author at all (neither in 1907 when Toklas met Stein, nor in 1933), and she was a (lesbian) woman writer creating difficult and obscure texts, two facts which, at that time at least, would be great obstacles for recognition as a genius.

The description of the first meeting between the two women is representative of many other incidents related in this book. Toklas as fictive narrator tells us nothing of her or Stein's emotions; instead, she concentrates on objects (e.g., Stein's coral brooch, p. 5), on furniture and paintings (pp. 9–10), or on Stein's enigmatic presence (sitting peacefully in a high-backed Italian Renaissance chair, p. 9). This "external perspective," as James E. Breslin calls it,[10] does not allow for the creation of an identity, an aim of traditional autobiography that Stein deeply mistrusts. Avoiding a focus on her inner life and placing herself in the midst of many Parisian celebrities together with Toklas, Stein creates a highly artful "portrait" of herself, similar to the one that Picasso paints of Stein: a seemingly remote figure sitting relaxed and peacefully in an armchair, either critically observing somebody/something or meditating.

This focus on Stein as if seen in/as a portrait and the narrative presence of Stein masquerading as Toklas undermines autobiographical writing in a creative way. On the one hand, the self is presented as something seen from the outside only. Thus, an essential part of the (autobiographical) self is missing. On the other hand, through language and the dialogic nature of the two selves, Toklas and Stein, Stein is very much alive and part of the life around her; she is not the static figure of a painting, nor is she provided with a fixed identity. Because the representation of an identity is denied, gender identity never seems to become an open issue. Stein's choice to have Toklas narrate "her" life already implies that this life became "theirs"; but it is a shared life depicted as a heterosexual marriage with traditional gender roles—Toklas as housewife and Stein as genius. Unlike *Everybody's Autobiography*, in which Stein is much more serious, open, and directly addressing gender issues, *The Autobiography of Alice B. Toklas* seems to deliberately deny that there might be a relationship between the genre of autobiography—which as a genre per se is questioned—and gender.

NOTES

1. Catharine R. Stimpson in her talk on *The Autobiography of Alice B. Toklas*, in the NEH Seminar on "Autobiographical Acts: Gender/Culture/Writing/Theory," conducted by Nancy K. Miller, New York, July 23, 1991.

2. Gertrude Stein, *The Autobiography of Alice B. Toklas* (New York: Random House, 1961), p. 252. All references in the text are from this edition.

3. See, for example, Stein's play *IIIIIIIIII*, in *Geography and Plays* (1922; reprint, New York: Haskell House, 1967), pp. 189–98.

4. Gertrude Stein, *Narration* (Chicago: University of Chicago Press, 1935), p. 45.

5. Quoted by Catharine Stimpson in her "Gertrude Stein and the Lesbian Lie," in *American Women's Autobiography: Fea(s)ts of Memory*, ed. Margo Culley (Madison: University of Wisconsin Press, 1992), p. 158; the quote by Hutcheon is from "Beginning to Theorize Postmodernism," *Textual Practice* 1/1 (Spring 1987): 25.

6. Laura Mulvey argues that in mainstream film, "woman" is displayed, represented, and viewed according to the voyeuristic gaze of the male subject. See "Visual Pleasure and Narrative Cinema," in *Feminism and Film Theory*, ed. Constance Penley (New York: Routledge, 1988), p. 62.

7. Richard Bridgman quotes from an unsigned letter by Stein to Allen Lane in which "some twenty photographs" are mentioned; Stein sent these to Harcourt Brace. See *Gertrude Stein in Pieces*, first footnote, p. 219. The first edition is *The Autobiography of Alice B. Toklas* (New York, 1933).

8. P. Adams Sitney, *Modernist Montage: The Obscurity of Vision in Cinema and Literature* (New York: Columbia University Press, 1990), p. 153.

9. See also Chessman's interpretation of the photograph; Chessman emphasizes the "mystery involved in such a doubling," in *The Public Is Invited to Dance*, pp. 61–62.

10. James E. Breslin, "Gertrude Stein and the Problems of Autobiography," *Georgia Review* 33, no. 4 (Winter 1979): 908.

8

The "I" in *Everybody's Autobiography*

Everybody's Autobiography is a kind of sequel to *The Autobiography of Alice B. Toklas*, yet it is quite different in voice, tone, and theme. Stein herself is the first-person narrator, and the comic, at times chatty tone of *The Autobiography of Alice B. Toklas* is replaced by a more serious, even sadder one. Stein addresses the problems of success and fame that the other book brought her, as well as the resulting writer's block. Philosophical views about American identity, an account of her trip to the United States and to England, and descriptions of her daily domestic life are the themes of this autobiography that claims to be "everybody's."

Denying that this is *her* autobiography and yet not disguising that she is the narrator, Stein again questions the notion of self and identity. Indeed, "identity always worries [her] and memory and eternity" (p. 115). Stein claims that real literary masterpieces must be created without relying on time and memory; therefore, to write an autobiography without memory as an orientation seems to be an impossible undertaking, and yet this is exactly what Stein attempts to do in this autobiography.

Stein begins *Everybody's Autobiography* by referring back to *The Autobiography of Alice B. Toklas*, which serves as a starting point to explore the question of autobiography and the novel. She presents her ideas by recounting a conversation she had with Dashiell Hammett in California. Stein questioned why men in the twentieth century mainly write about themselves instead of inventing men. Women, she says,

never could invent women they always made the women be themselves seen splendidly or sadly or heroically or beautifully or despairingly or gently. . . . From Charlotte Brontë to George Eliot and many years later this was true. Now in the twentieth century it is the men who do it. (p. 5)

Stein seems to agree with Hammett who explains that men concentrate on themselves because they lack confidence. Although Stein does not comment on Hammett's answer, her rendering of this whole conversation at the beginning of "everybody's autobiography" is an implicit statement about women's writing as traditionally having been autobiographical. Novels by women writers, she seems to imply, were always closer to autobiography than novels written by men. Thus, Stein, who deeply mistrusts the novel form, perceives similarities between her foremothers Brontë and Eliot, both in terms of genre and gender. It is interesting to note that Stein was especially fond of Eliot's writings; as a young woman she seemed to identify with Maggie Tulliver, the tragic female protagonist of *Mill on the Floss*.[1] Emphasizing that fictive invention belongs to the nineteenth century and to a male tradition, and yet, at the same time, questioning an adequate presentation of the self, Stein must look for new forms. Her radical statement "[a]nything is an autobiography" (p. 5) does not relieve her of the problems of how to deal with identity; on the contrary, the belief in autobiographical writing makes her focus on a self that cannot be restricted to the author's. Her own self and the selves of the others, that is, everybody's self, are intertwined through the act of writing.

For Stein, writing necessarily entails the confrontation with identity:

The thing is like this, it is all a question of identity. It is all a question of the outside being outside and the inside being inside. As long as the outside does not put a value on you it remains outside but when it does put a value on you then it gets inside or rather if the outside puts a value on you then all your inside gets to be outside. (p. 47)

This passage describes the effects that the success of *The Autobiography of Alice B. Toklas* had on Stein: she had a writing block for a few months because her inside was turned outside, that is, the public (the outside) valued her and thus her inside was exposed and affected; it could no longer be productive and creative. This "inside" normally contains "words that had to be written" (p. 64), but now, being famous and attracting attention, she feels "[n]othing inside [her] needed to be written" and "there was no word inside [her]" (p. 64). For Stein, not writing means that she begins to worry about identity since she "had always been [her] because [she] had words that had to be written inside [her]" (p. 64). Writing enables her to have an identity. Thus, having a self can only be achieved through writing. How, then, can she write an autobiography if this very self that she is going to write about is being created in the process of writing?

The paradox inherent in this question belongs to the difficulty of writing one's self because this self is continuously subject to change. Unlike many autobiographers, who seem to be able to write about their lives—and selves—retrospectively, Stein is both attracted and troubled by this phenomenon. Her way of resolving the intricacies of the represented self is to focus on the "now" of the self, on the moment of writing. Since the self is only created through writing, she as its author and creator is bound to concentrate on the moment. Although Stein's trip to the United States is a major topic in *Everybody's*

Autobiography, looking back at this event is a matter of the "now." A consequence of this predominance of the present is the digressive structure of this autobiography. The digressions relate to the moment of writing or to events that happened very recently. Examples like "[j]ust the other day . . ." (p. 116), "I just met a French woman . . . and I was telling her . . . " (p. 121), "yesterday I went to the studio of a man . . . " (p. 178), or "I find out just today . . ." (p. 210) abound when Stein tells us about her trip to the States, compelling the writer's present to become the focus of this autobiography. Furthermore, the emphasis on the "now" brings the process of writing into the discussion, which, in turn, is concerned with identity.

It is not surprising then that Stein's autobiography constantly shifts between events that happened in the past and her ideas and thoughts about writing. The combination of these two discourses makes the reader aware of the impact of time because the past is not graspable without the perceiving mind of the "now." Moreover, this orientation to the moment is intertwined with the creation of an identity at the moment of writing. Stein's occupation with the past through and with the present is the only way of exploring one's self. Therefore, Toklas, who had her own narrative voice in the first autobiography, is now Stein's companion in a more direct and established way. Stein does not "lie" about her authorship anymore, or about her relationship with Toklas, although there are no explicit references to her lesbianism. For Stein, identity is still a problem to be written about constantly, but it is not something to play a game with as in the first autobiography. The shifting between past and present is necessary in order to write about one's life, and always includes others as well. This relation between past and present also takes place between Stein as author and her companion Toklas, and between the lives of others. The result both is and is not "everybody's autobiography" because not everybody could have written this autobiography, but the many ordinary events and daily occurrences may indeed include everybody.[2] Identity, everybody, and time are thus interrelated through the act of writing.

The act of writing and "the autobiographical act"[3] become one and the same. Stein not only undermines autobiographical writing by pretending to write for everybody, that is, to take everybody's position, she also demonstrates that for her, autobiographical writing includes everybody. The capacity to write for everybody and yet write autobiography can only be found in a genius. To be a genius is something that Stein explores again and again in the course of her autobiography—and also in other works—because only a genius can produce a masterpiece, which is what her autobiography is meant to be. A genius and his or her product are always concerned about time, but they "have no more time than they have identity."[4] Therefore, it is the present moment that is essential, and memory must be eliminated when creating a masterpiece because it confuses the writer. Although this masterpiece is independent of time, it is nevertheless the present that plays an essential role because it is the present moment at which the writer is writing without remembering.

The question remains how Stein can write about her trip to the United States without relying on her memory. Stein's method of writing about her ideas of the moment also enable her to write down her associations with the past; thoughts of the moment and about events of the past are brought together and no longer differentiated according to a chronological pattern. The self of the present determines what the author tells us about the (her) past, and it is not chronology, that is, time, that controls the writing. Autobiography is writing about a self that is being created through this very act. The claim to present one's life retrospectively and to give a more or less true account of past events is obviously contested.

Instead of relating past events according to a chronological pattern, Stein explores philosophical questions triggered by associations with the past. The topics range from identity, time, eternity, and death to genius, masterpieces, and fathers. Although Stein's concern about fathers does not seem to be a predominant theme, it must be seen in relation with the others. Her observations about fathers reveal a more general criticism of the position of fathers, that is, of the patriarchal institution. The following passage begins with her personal experience as a fatherless girl (after her father died), and then describes "fathering" in the public and political realm. Both the private and the public realm suggest that "fathers are depressing" and that "too much fathering [is] going on just now" (p. 133):

Then our life without a father began a very pleasant one. I have been thinking a lot about fathers any kind of fathers. . . . And fathers come up and fathers go down. That is natural enough when nobody has had fathers they begin to long for them and then when everybody has had fathers they begin to long to do without them. Sometimes barons and dukes are fathers and then kings come to be fathers and churchmen come to be fathers and then comes a period like the eighteenth century a nice period when everybody has had enough of anybody being a father to them and then gradually capitalists and trade unionists become fathers and which goes on to communists and dictators, just now everybody has a father, perhaps the twenty-first century like the eighteenth century will be a nice time when everybody forgets to be a father or to have been one. (p. 142)

The enumeration of political and public figures such as barons, kings, or communists who are fathers insinuates that there is a close link between the figure of the father and the male figure holding public office and exercising a certain power. Stein is quite explicit about her critical stance toward this patriarchal system that seems to have very negative effects. Referring to contemporary political leaders ("just now," and "there is father Mussolini and father Hitler" p. 133), she unmasks the (dismal) political situation as being patriarchal. Stein connects her (female) autobiography, which does not respect traditional (male) patterns, with her criticism of patriarchy. She abnegates both the form of chronological autobiography and the patriarchal institution because both are subject to a generational pattern marked by fathers and sons. Stein presents herself through the autobiographical act, the "masterpiece," as a woman independent of fathers, be they political fathers or literary forefathers.

Stein's focus on the moment and her aim to describe it without looking back to the past enables her to free herself from "depressing fathers." In the same way that she had to distance herself from her own country and forefathers when she settled down in Paris, she distances herself from any prescribing fathering that might set limits to the creation of her self through writing. The ending of *Everybody's Autobiography* expresses her concentration on the "now" and her belief in the moment of writing without looking back: "perhaps I am not even I even if my little dog knows me but anyway I like what I have and now it is today" (p. 318). The indeterminateness of the self remains, but it is free of limits and is being created anew again and again. Stein's autobiography could indeed be everybody's because the self is neither fixed nor described according to a chronological pattern, and yet Stein's female self is omnipresent as it is inscribed from moment to moment. The gender of this autobiography is obvious, whereas its genre is not: Stein's text is not recognizable as autobiography anymore. Gender surpasses genre.

NOTES

1. See also Bridgman's comment on Stein and George Eliot in *Gertrude Stein in Pieces* (New York: Oxford University Press, 1970), pp. 24–26.

2. For possible explanations of Stein's title, see Monika Hoffmann's chapter "Der Titel von *Everybody's Autobiography*," *Gertrude Steins Autobiographien: The Autobiography of Alice B. Toklas und Everybody's Biography* (Frankfurt am Main: Peter Lang, 1992), pp. 293–97. Hoffmann concludes that "everybody" as a representative of everyday occurrences is the subject matter of autobiography, and therefore everybody is addressed through this book (p. 297).

3. See Nancy K. Miller's book *Getting Personal: Feminist Occasions and Other Autobiographical Acts* (New York: Routledge, 1991).

4. Gertrude Stein, "What Are Master-Pieces" in *What Are Masterpieces*, p. 91.

9

Wars I Have Seen: Seeing and Telling Through the I/Eye

The title *Wars I Have Seen* raises the specter of war memoirs with descriptions of battles or frightful war experiences, but Stein's book neither tells us of battles nor about dreadful atrocities. Stein describes her and Toklas's daily life in occupied France, characterized by the search for food and wood, and dealings with officials, soldiers, and the maquis. The account is very ethnographic: strategies for obtaining eggs or milk, the reason why the villagers only wore wooden shoes, how their families were for or against the maquis. Life during wartime, it seems, is nothing extraordinary because, as Stein emphasizes, everybody is concerned about "small things": "it is not like it was there is nothing to be curious about except small things, food and the weather."[1] Nevertheless, Stein is very curious about these "small things."

Stein's account of this daily life also includes philosophical and historical themes; she thinks about war in general and how, as a child, she read books about wars and how a war was going on inside her. She pays special attention to adolescence, which was a difficult time for her, and she uses the analogy of war to illustrate its struggles:

It was when I was between twelve and seventeen that I went through the dark and dreadful days of adolescence, in which predominated the fear of death, not so much of death as of dissolution, and naturally is war like that. It is and it is not. One really can say that in war-time there is death death and death but is there dissolution. I wonder. May that not be one of the reasons among so many others why wars go on, and why particularly adolescents need it. (p. 8)

Stein's use of the analogy of the war to describe a painful and terrible experience in her own life is indicative of her way of combining inner and outer experience. Living through two wars and looking back to her adolescent years makes her aware of similar emotions: To her the fear of death is the same during

a war as one has when growing up. Although she depicts the small things during
wartime, fear is nevertheless omnipresent, and thus, looking back to her childhood, she draws this parallel. Bridgman's explanation that Stein tried "to
account for the war by finding an analogy for it in her personal life"[2] does not
consider her way of using analogies in order to combine the present with the
past. This kind of combination is similar to the associative way of writing
dominant in *Everybody's Autobiography*. Therefore, it is always the present that
draws Stein's attention, and yet more than a description of actual life is given.
Philosophical exploration goes hand in hand with domestic affairs, or with an
account of the momentary situation of the war.

When Stein and Toklas are directly confronted with the effects of the war,
such as having to put up German soldiers at their house in Culoz, or thinking
about leaving for Switzerland, Stein keeps her attention more or less on the
present. Her account reads like a diary with entries of single days. Temporal
specifications such as "and now," "this morning just before dawn," "today," or
"to-night" enhance the actuality of these wartime days. When the end of the war
is near, and each day brings new events, philosophical observations rarely sur-
face. Stein's descriptions of the turbulence and excitement of these last days of
the war read like a diary, but they could also have been written for a newspaper
report. The seriousness and also sadness of the first part have disappeared, and
Stein now expresses her excitement and joy about the end of the war. With the
arrival of the Americans in Culoz, Stein wants to conclude her memoirs, as she
has always planned: "What a day what a day of days, I always did say that I
would end this book with the first American that came to Culoz, and to-day oh
happy day yesterday and to-day, the first of September 1944. There have been
six of them in the house, two of them stayed the night" (pp. 161–62).

Wars I Have Seen concludes on this jubilant, and also quite patriotic, tone.
The last pages are very different compared with the account of the daily routine
of war days, and considering the relief and joy, patriotism for America is not
surprising. But like the other autobiographies, *Wars I Have Seen* ends with the
emphasis on the present: "And so we are back in Paris. . . . Yes, I walk around
Paris" (p. 175).

As this autobiography portrays Stein's war years and her daily life, Stein's
"I" is not as crucial as her "eye" that describes what is going on around her. And
yet, writing what she *sees* every day includes her own self, but it is a self that is
manifest through the continuous writing, and thus is not fixed at all. Moreover,
it is always closely connected with Toklas, as demonstrated by the frequent use
of the pronoun "we" instead of "I." In *Wars I Have Seen* Stein presents a self
that is always in relation to everyday events and the people she meets; as in
Everybody's Autobiography, others are as important as her own self. Therefore,
identity is undetermined and always subject to constant change. The personal
pronoun "I" in the title is less prominent in the text than the participle "seen"
because it is the seeing that is transformed into writing and thereby changes the
"I." For Stein, writing autobiography is seeing lives and not so much telling
one's life. The genre autobiography includes biography as well because the lives

of others are both alluring and necessary to Stein. *Four in America* is a convincing example of the relationship between autobiography and biography. Gender plays an essential role in mediating between the two in a work where Stein as the woman artist sees and transforms the lives of famous men.

NOTES

1. Gertrude Stein, *Wars I Have Seen* (London: B. T. Batsford, 1945), p. 65. All page references given in the text are from this edition.

2. Robert Bridgman, *Gertrude Stein in Pieces* (New York: Oxford University Press, 1970), p. 327.

10

Foreign America: *Four in America* and Gertrude Stein

> I have been writing the portraits of Four In America, trying to write Grant, and Wilbur Wright and Henry James and Washington do other things than they did do so as to try to find out just what it is that what happens has to do with what is. (*LA*, p. 206)

Gertrude Stein calls her descriptions of the four Americans "portraits," that is, she gives her work a generic label. Moreover, she states as her philosophical interest the relationship between what happens and what is. "Recreating" four historical figures in order to find out about the relationship between event (what happens) and status quo (what is)[1] seems a bold undertaking. Yet, given Stein's subversive use of form(s) and figure(s), we must expect "re- and excreation." As mentioned at the beginning, Stein means the "recreation of the word"[2] and coins the word "excreate."[3] Both re-creating and "excreating" signal change, process, and metamorphosis. For Stein, writing about "what is" always entails writing about change and process; in examining these she also creates new genres or deconstructs traditional ones. Such creation or deconstruction of genres is closely connected with issues of gender: Stein's re-creation of four American *male* historical icons is not based on biographical facts or achievements but on her own ideas on creativity as a *female* artist.

Although an expatriate for most of her life, Gertrude Stein was always concerned with American history, American geography, and, above all, American character, which she approaches through autobiography. It is not clear whether *The Geographical History of America or The Relation of Human Nature to The Human Mind* is a text dealing with American history, a philosophical inquiry into the American mind, or an autobiography. *Four in America* is also a text that defies generic classification, although Stein uses the term "portrait." Commenting on this work in the second of her four lectures given at the University of Chicago in 1935, she speaks of "the history of some one if his name had not been the name he had."[4] Stein uses "portrait" and "history" in reference to *Four in America* without further distinction. She comes up with these "genres" because, as we know, a coherent narrative cannot be told: "moving is in every direction beginning and ending is not really exciting."[5] Although disrupting linearity, Stein does not seem to be totally marginalized by patriarchal society.[6] Indeed, it seems as if Stein is one of the very few women who "speaks" and "writes" but does not identify with patriarchal values, that is, she defies Father Time, yet does not remain outside history or politics, which are determined by paternal, linear time. Lonely and almost obnoxiously she writes according to her own beliefs, yet is always in a dialogue with other writers and artists during her lifetime.

Stein's subversive concept of time relates also to Kristeva's formulations in "Women's Time," in which she connects cyclical time and monumental time to female subjectivity. Cyclical time is characterized by repetition, cycles, and gestation, whereas monumental time refers to time as it appears in mythology (e.g., Kronos) or Christianity (resurrection). Both cyclical time and monumental time are, according to Kristeva, opposed to linear time, the time of history,[7] which is also inherent in language, in the sequence of words. As mentioned before, Stein's breaking of such a sequence and her insistence on repetition and circularity illustrate that she does not succumb to linear time even if she writes about "history," as in *Four in America*.

As Stein is not bound to linear time, she can change everything and everybody in order to find out what *is*—as she does in *Four in America*. The four historical figures—Ulysses S. Grant, Wilbur Wright, Henry James, and George Washington—occupy a special place in American history. All were creative in a particular field, and this creativity in connection with American character attracted Gertrude Stein. By assigning professions other than their historical ones to these four heroes, she endeavors to probe the question of American identity and creativity in general:

> If Ulysses S. Grant had been a religious leader who was to become a saint what would he have done.
> If the Wright brothers had been artists that is painters what would they have done.
> If Henry James had been a general what would he have had to do.
> If General Washington had been a writer that is a novelist what would he do.[8]

The first speculation of the four hypotheses opens the way for Stein to ponder the relation between name and person. Her focus is on identity. She is convinced that "the given name or the Christian name does or do denote character and career" (p. 3). That is why, in her view, Grant's original Christian name Hiram (which he later changed) makes him a religious leader. Stein demonstrates the irrational attribution of certain characteristics to a certain person because of a certain name, a process we know from children who easily identify names with very definite qualities of persons they know. Moreover, she links this "knowing" about names with religious belief and tries to answer the ever returning question What is religion? Her answers do not develop according to a logical pattern; instead, she begins to discuss American religion. She juxtaposes American religion with European religion, concluding that "American religion" is "open" because it has no sky:

You see in European religion they need a wind and they need window but not I, not American religion, not I. They need no wind or window or sky because there is no wind no window and no sky, not in American religion not in American war, not in America before or after war. (p. 30)

This passage with the typical Steinian explanations, which are "simple through complication,"[9] describes American religion as something that cannot be localized or determined; according to Stein it is, like American war and America, not planned, organized, led, or determined by expectation or memory. In order to understand these characteristics of vastness, vagueness, and "openness," we must take into consideration Gertrude Stein's life in France: Although an American, she was confronted with daily life in France, which must have appeared more organized to her than life in America.[10] But what has this to do with the original question about religion?

Stein tackles such a complex question by making observations not necessarily related to its background. How does Stein arrive at these observations, which, in the end, sound like possible answers to the question at issue? This process, which encompasses both reader and writer, is essential for Stein's creative power. In his introduction to *Four in America*, Thornton Wilder points out that this book "is *being written* before our eyes. . . . She gives us the process" (p. xiv, his emphasis). Moreover, Stein's mistrust of a generally accepted meaning of a word makes her repeat a word, modify it, and finally arrive at the point where it may carry just the opposite meaning it had at the outset. Or, in what Thornton Wilder calls "compressions" (p. xxi), an overwhelming summary or a wholly unexpected new topic may throw a reader off balance, if she or he is looking for a gradual, linear development of an idea. Stein's hypothetical questions trigger off other questions, which have more to do with Stein's own creativity and "American-ness" than with the titular subject of *Four in America*—four icons of American culture and history.

This emphasis on process is linked to Stein's concept of time: Not linear but repetitive and circular time shape the presentation of these four heroes. Stein as female artist is the creatress of the "history" of these four men, and she does not yield to time as imposed by their (male) history or by their biographies. Therefore, the literary form for this "re-creation" is "excreative" as well; it is both a "blurring of genres" and a creation of other forms, namely the portrait and the landscape. I shall discuss the latter in connection with the last section of the book, that on George Washington.

The second section on Wilbur Wright also emphasizes the impact of a Christian name, as did the first on Grant, but then goes on to explore the relationship between aviation and painting. The man who creates the flying machine and flies in it is part of the creative act in a manner similar to the cubist painter: The flier traverses space itself, which offers him shifting perspectives, while the cubist painter tries to present an object in space as seen from various perspectives. Stein is fascinated by the fact that Wright "*sees* when he moves," "how he moves," and "*sees* moving" (p. 96, my emphasis): Seeing is essential for Stein, and she emphasizes this ability with regard to painter and actor.

Richard Bridgman complains that Stein does not make the similarities between flier, painter, and actor sufficiently clear for the reader. He criticizes her for this lack of explanatory capability;[11] I would argue that the abundance of direct, almost pleading addresses to the reader or to Lizzie[12] compel us to witness Stein's creative act. Like incantations, the pleas try to persuade the reader and/or Lizzie to be attentive: "I tell you I will tell you. While and awhile and I will I will tell you" (p. 87). "Oh Lizzie do you do you understand. I wish you would because I do and I wish oh how I wish that you would too. Lizzie do you understand" (p. 88). "Listen to me listen to this" (p. 93). "Now then hear then what I say of them" (p. 96). "Can you do you see" (p. 97). This dialogic element in a "history" about American heroes subverts the so-called objective approach we would expect of a presentation of such figures. We not only witness the author's "circular" search for clarity but also participate in her linguistic search for creation.

Although the Henry James section focuses on James the general, James the writer and Stein the writer are at the center of it all. Stein and James never met, nor did they correspond with each other. In 1914, Stein obviously tried to arrange a meeting, but James declined to receive any visitors at that time.[13] All the same, James turns up in Stein's works in many ways, and seems to occupy a prominent place in her ideas about literary creativity. As early as 1916 and 1918, Stein wrote two very short pieces about James, a portrait called "Henry and I," and a so-called poem "James Is Nervous."[14] Both pay tribute to James as a writer. In *The Autobiography of Alice B. Toklas*, Stein denies having been influenced by James in her early years, yet she calls him "the only nineteenth century writer who being an american felt the method of the twentieth century" (*ABT*, p. 78). In an interview in 1946, a few months before her death, she calls James "a forerunner" with regard to composing literary texts:

You see I tried to convey the idea of each part of a composition being as important as the whole. It was the first time in any language that anyone had used that idea of composition in literature. Henry James had a slight inkling of it and was in some senses a forerunner, while in my case I made it stay on the page quite composed. You see he made it sort of like an atmosphere, and it was not solely the realism of the characters but the realism of the composition which was the important thing, the realism of the composition of my thoughts.[15]

Stein's "re-creation" of Henry James the *general* not only throws light on Stein's view of James's writing methods but also points to the issue of gender because Stein implicitly applies the analogy of the general to her own writing. Thus, the masculinist criteria we associate with "general" are used by a female writer whose work challenges phallogocentric discourse in very radical and complex ways. The presentation of her autobiographical self, which is clearly recognizable in *Four in America*, is often male-identified. Therefore, a reading of Stein's fictional biography of James must provide some explanations for this "transposition of gender."[16]

The section on Henry James begins with a comment on the difference between Shakespeare's plays and his sonnets. The plays, Stein writes, "were written as they were written," and the sonnets "were written as they were going to be written" (p. 120). The question about the relationship between accident (what happens) and coincidence (what is going to happen) is crucial in Stein's meditations on the problems of writing. The sonnets are coincidental in the sense that they were going to happen, that is they were carefully planned. Stein became aware of this difference when she wrote the poems *Before the Flowers of Friendship Faded Friendship Faded*, which she began as a translation of poems in French by her friend Georges Hugnet. She realized "that words come out differently if there is no recognition as the words are forming because recognition had already taken place."[17] She combined writing about what she already knew and writing about the process that entails new knowledge. Stein worries about the clarity of her explanations regarding Shakespeare's plays and sonnets because she addresses the reader with apologetic pleas such as "This sounds mixed but it is not and it is so important. Oh dear it is so important" (p. 129). The Steinian sentence "I am I not any longer when I see," which, according to her, "is at the bottom of all creative activity" (p. 119), is more revealing; it deals with the question of the self that perceives and thus undergoes a change by this very perception.

Stein's statement about the two ways of writing, namely "writing what you are writing" and "writing what you are going to be writing" (p. 122), which correspond to the pair accident/coincidence, seeks to elucidate the principal dynamics inherent in the composition of a text: writing as a process and writing as a product that is being received. Therefore, the two ways of writing should be combined because a writer writes what she or he intends to write, but also writes what must be written because it may develop from the already written. With regard to James, Stein states that he knew how to combine these two ways of writing: "He saw he could write both ways at once" (p. 133). In Stein's opinion, this strategy of composing makes James a general: His writing satisfies a plan ("writing what you are writing") as well as its execution ("writing what you are going to be writing"). According to Stein, James, like herself, knew how to combine creation and perception, writing and listening to the written word(s). Her metaphor of the general seems even more appropriate given James's fascination for generals and warfare on his deathbed, imagining himself to be Napoleon.[18] Stein herself also seems to like the idea of being a general: "and anyway what am I I am an American, Alice says a civil war general in retirement, perhaps."[19] Both writer and general must combine the capabilities of planning and improvising simultaneously.

Stein's concern about (an) audience is tightly interwoven with the act of writing: "When you are writing who hears what you are writing" (p. 121). In the section on James, her observations on her own and James's writing methods become intertwined with what she calls audience. In a letter to Thornton Wilder in 1934 she is quite explicit about the relationship between James and her pre-occupation with audience: "I am and have been very full of meditations about direct and indirect vision, and the relation between the writer and an audience either actual or not actual, I have just been writing about four Americans and one of them Henry James has cleared up a lot of things for me that is in trying to put him down."[20]

Stein's playful approach to a hypothetical biography of James the general allows her to ask the reader/listener again and again whether a general wins a battle and if he does, how he does it. Thus, Stein lets us participate in her searching creation of James's biography. Devising a strategy that necessitates listening, the very strategy she attributes to James's profession as a general, she demonstrates the two ways of writing: "Henry James is a combination of the two ways of writing and that makes him a general a general who does something. Listen to it" (p. 137). Thus, not only Henry James but also Stein combines the two ways of writing: The pronoun "it" refers to her creation of James, although James himself can do "it" (the two ways of writing), too.

Stein's creative biography of James furthermore introduces *three* Jameses. This emphasis on more than one identity is fundamental to Stein's concept of writing, which is always dialogic, multivocal, and open. In her last lecture on *Narration* she provides a philosophical explanation of the process between writer and text:

That is what mysticism is, that is what the Trinity is, that is what marriage is, the absolute conviction that in spite of knowing anything about everything about how any one is never really feeling what any other one is really feeling that after all after all three are one and two are one. One is not one because one is always two that is one is always coming to a recognition of what the one who is one is writing that is telling.[21]

There is no telling where "one" begins and where "one" ends; writing itself already involves more than one self because the self of the writer changes through the act of creation and through an audience. This numeric logic of writing and listening is applied by Stein to James: "That is what most writing is. Sometimes two of three do listen and do hear. . . . Now in the case of Henry James listen in the case of Henry James all of them all three of them listened" (p. 136). The pronoun "them" is never exactly specified; I suggest it refers to both audience in general and to the artist in particular, who, hearing him/herself, is in a dialogue with his/her own words.

Stein's designation of the "three Jameses" (p. 139) also alludes to the three biological Jameses—to father Henry and his sons William (Stein's professor and tutor at Radcliffe) and Henry. A third reason for the presence of the triadic Jameses may be James's own tripartite autobiography, *A Small Boy and Others*, *Notes of a Son and Brother*, and *The Middle Years*, which Stein had most probably read. Thus, his autobiography and her biography of James are connected: Stein's portrait of James can also be read as an indirect comment on James's autobiography.

The metaphor of marriage used by Stein to explain the multivocal essence of writing and listening can also be applied to *The Autobiography of Alice B. Toklas* because her lesbian relationship is presented as a heterosexual marriage. The metaphor of marriage also suggests a marriage of voices, dialogue, writing, and listening, which, as is the case in many works by Stein, can create erotic pleasure. Speaking about James, Stein is eager to emphasize James's unmarried status: "It is of great importance that Henry James was never married" (p. 143), or "Now I wish to say generously why he was never married either as a general or as a man" (p. 142). Although Stein implicitly links James's autobiography with her own, there is a striking difference: Marriage is not the center of James's vision, neither concretely nor metaphorically. Instead, his autobiography focuses on father, son, and brother, and on his cousin Minnie Temple, whom he *did not* marry.[22] Considering the sexual or, rather, homoerotic implications of a story such as "The Beast in the Jungle,"[23] Stein's insistence on James's unmarried status strikingly contrasts with her own presentation of partnership in *The Autobiography of Alice B. Toklas*.

In James's autobiography it is indeed "Mr. Ba(t)chelor"—to borrow the name of Thackeray's narrator in *Lovel the Widower*—who looks back on his life as a boy and young man. Unlike Stein, who presents marriage both in her life (with Toklas) and in her point of view (Toklas's fictive narrative stance), James concentrates on himself and on family relationships without giving up the control over his own narrative voice. Nevertheless, Henry James is a general because he combines the two ways of writing—planning and improvising.

Stein's portrait of James is a picture that is uniquely her own: it includes biographical reference to James as much as it expresses Stein's autobiographical self; it enables her to position herself with James as a general in the line of male creative figures, an understandable and also shrewd strategy for a lesbian writer of her time. She, like James and the three others of *Four in America*, belongs to the history of American creativity, although she, also like James, has remained a "foreign" American. Both James and Stein wrote American literature as expatriates.

When Stein tries to characterize American literature, she is eager to discuss the construction of paragraphs. Paragraphs, she insists, are emotional, but sentences are not.[24] Sentences are structured according to rules, and emotions have to yield to the structure of a sentence, whereas a paragraph, a composition of sentences, can be constructed more freely and associatively. American literature is, according to Stein, something that is "without any connection" because a structured American daily life does not exist compared to the English daily island life. Therefore, only an American like James could find the form of "the disembodied way of disconnecting something from anything and anything from something," and "his whole paragraph was detached what it said from what it did, what it was from what it held" (*LA*, p. 53). We are reminded of James's own observation in *The Ivory Tower* about "the American want of correspondence" and about "a special radiance of disconnection."[25] Stein sees James as one who prepared the twentieth century, which, as she states, is represented by America. But she went further than James, and "had to do more with the paragraph than ever had been done. . . . and I kept breaking the paragraph down, and everything down to commence again with not connecting with the daily anything" (*LA*, p. 54). Stein attributes to James a knowledge of the disconnecting risks of modern life, which needed new forms of representation. Indeed, only two Americans physically disconnected from America could create such new forms in their American mother tongue. But Stein considers herself to be the one who does "the important literary thinking" (*GHA*, p. 182), and her creation of Henry James is again a demonstration of how she as a writer is creative.

George Washington, the general of the last section, is a novelist in Stein's hypothetical history of the "four in America." Her presentation of Washington carries surprising generic labels: "Scenery and George Washington a Novel or a Play" (p. 161). For Stein, scenery or landscape, which have the same meaning for her, belong to her concept of a play.[26] She sees a revealing similarity between a landscape and a play: like a landscape that remains the same for the onlooker who contemplates it, a play should not develop a story; Stein requires the same "stillness" from a play. But why is the section on George Washington connected with scenery or landscape, and thus also with a play? Some conclusions can be drawn from the date and circumstances of its composition.

Stein and Toklas's house in Bilignin overlooked the landscape of the Bugey, and this scenery shaped Stein's view and perception in various respects. She often meditated while looking over the valley below her, and her perception of this landscape pervades the writing composed during the time at Bilignin. "Scenery and George Washington" was probably written during such a stay at Bilignin. The reference to "autumn scenery" (p. 161) also sets the season of the year.[27] This section was published separately in 1932, and then incorporated later in *Four in America*. George Washington appealed to Stein because he represented American history and the beginning of a nation.

But Stein does not present the father of this nation as a remote historical figure; instead, she familiarizes Washington by bringing him (after the fog has disappeared) into a serene autumn scene equivalent to the one experienced by the author. George Washington is "written" into this landscape as if he were a frequent guest there. Moreover, Stein's presumption that he is a novelist allows her to ask again what a novel is:

> It is true that George Washington never came through.
> That is what a novel is.
> He knew.
> He knew what a novel is.
> It is true.
> How true.
> Through to you. (p. 221)

Although Washington the novelist seems to know what a novel is, the author of *Four in America* does not; she only knows that a novel cannot bring anything "[t]hrough to you" because "there is always a sequel" (p. 199). Only for her nonsequential presentation of Washington could she acknowledge that she came "through to you." That is the only valid statement a writer like Stein can make, a writer who mistrusts any sequence or category, be it historical, fictional, or generic.

Stein uses a third term in her range of generic labels besides "landscape" and "play"; after a few pages on the autumn scenery, which are divided into short sections called "pages," she begins a new chapter titled "Or a History of the United States of America" (p. 167). Thus, the subtitle "Scenery and George Washington a Novel or a Play" must be read together with this additional designation. These three quite different terms totally disrupt our generic expectations. Neither "novel," "play," nor "history" can be applied to this text according to common definitions. The main section titled "Or a History of the United States" contains long passages about novel writing and is not historical in any usual respect. Stein's division into "volumes" further undermines our notions of order because some volumes are quite long, while others consist of only one line: "Volume III: If they knew what a novel is, how do they know it" (p. 174); there is no intelligible reason for this uneven division unless to unsettle the principle of division and coherence.

Stein's text about these four influential male Americans is neither a history nor a fictional presentation; it is the creative process of the female American artist Gertrude Stein, who, in the end, is "foreign (in) America." Therefore, genres such as landscape, novel, play, or history cannot be defined or clearly distinguished from each other if the writer is writing about writing and about the difficulties of defining a novel. Stein writing about the difficulties and differences in and of writing will be the topic of Part 4.

NOTES

1. Charles Caramello speaks of "event" and "consequence" when he explains Stein's "what happens" and "what is." See his "Reading Gertrude Stein Reading Henry James, or Eros Is Eros Is Eros Is Eros," *Henry James Review* 6, no. 3 (Spring 1985): 186.

2. See note 51 of my introduction.

3. See note 39 of my first chapter.

4. Gertrude Stein, *Narration* (Chicago: University of Chicago Press, 1935), p. 29.

5. Stein, *Narration*, p. 19.

6. As mentioned in my introduction, Kristeva refers to women writers who became so marginalized that they committed suicide (e.g., Sylvia Plath, Marina Tsvetayeva).

7. Julia Kristeva, "Women's Time" [1979], in *The Kristeva Reader*, ed. Toril Moi, pp. 191–92.

8. Gertrude Stein, *Four in America* (New Haven, CT: Yale University Press, 1947), p. 1. All subsequent page references refer to this edition and are cited in the text.

9. Gertrude Stein, "A Transatlantic Interview 1946," *A Primer for the Gradual Understanding of Gertrude Stein*, ed. Robert Bartlett Haas (Los Angeles: Black Sparrow Press, 1971), p. 34.

10. See, for example, *Lectures in America*, pp. 53–54.

11. Richard Bridgman, *Gertrude Stein in Pieces* (New York: Oxford University Press, 1970), p. 240.

12. This addressee is also used in *Blood on the Dining-Room Floor*.

13. See James Mellow, *Charmed Circle: Gertrude Stein and Company* (New York: Praeger Publisher, 1974), p. 212.

14. Gertrude Stein, *Painted Lace*, pp. 273–74; *Bee Time Vine and Other Pieces [1913–1927]*, p. 208.

15. Gertrude Stein, "A Transatlantic Interview 1946," pp. 15–16.

16. Catharine R. Stimpson, "Gertrude Stein and the Transposition of Gender," in *The Poetics of Gender*, ed. Nancy K. Miller (New York: Columbia University Press, 1986), pp. 1–18.

17. Gertrude Stein, *Narration*, p. 52.

18. Henry James, *The Complete Notebooks*, ed. Leon Edel and Lyall H. Powers (New York: Oxford University Press, 1987), pp. 582–84.

19. In a letter to Henry McBride, May 22, 1929.

20. Ray Lewis White, ed. *Sherwood Anderson/Gertrude Stein: Correspondence and Personal Essays* (Chapel Hill: University of North Carolina Press, 1972), p. 85.

21. Gertrude Stein, *Narration*, p. 57.

22. Charles Caramello comments on this fact in his illuminating article "Reading Gertrude Stein Reading Henry James, or Eros Is Eros Is Eros Is Eros," *Henry James Review* 6, no. 3 (Spring 1985): 192.

23. See Eve Sedgwick's interpretation of this story, "The Beast in the Closet: James and the Writing of Homosexual Panic," in *Speaking of Gender*, ed. Elaine Showalter (New York: Routledge, 1989), pp. 243–68.

24. See Gertrude Stein, *Lectures in America*, p. 48; and *How to Write*, p. 23.

25. Henry James, *The Ivory Tower* (New York: Scribner's, 1917), p. 78. Donald Sutherland refers to this passage in his *Gertrude Stein: A Biography of Her Work* (New Haven, CT: Yale University Press, 1951), p. 93, n. 31.

26. Stein uses the two words indiscriminately: "autumn landscape," "autumn scenery." See *FIA*, pp. 163–64.

27. For a comment on the date of composition of "Scenery and George Washington," see Ulla Dydo, "Gertrude Stein: Composition as Meditation," in *Gertrude Stein and the Making of Literature*, ed. Shirley Neuman and Ira B. Nadel (London, 1988), p. 59, n. 7.

IV

Detection and Meditation

11

The Subject of Detection: *Blood on the Dining-Room Floor*

Stein's "murder mystery" *Blood on the Dining-Room Floor*[1] was written after her writing block in the summer of 1933. Writing a detective novel seems to have been a way of overcoming the problems she was confronted with after her success with *The Autobiography of Alice B. Toklas*. Stein chose a genre she had never used before. We know that Stein was eager to experiment with new genres and that she used similar themes in various different genres. The events that took place during the summer of 1933 became her detective story, but also entered other pieces such as "A Waterfall and A Piano" and "Is Dead."[2] In *Everybody's Autobiography* there are various references to the strange events, and Stein explains how they occupied her mind: "It is funny how often I have tried to tell the story of that summer, I have tried to tell it again and again" (*EA*, p. 52).

The difficulty of writing about these events and the form of the detective novel seem to be related. In order to explore this relationship, these events must first be described and analyzed.[3] The most eminent as well as most tragic incident was Madame Pernollet's death. Madame Pernollet, who was the owner of a hotel together with her husband, was found one morning in the cement courtyard; she died a few days later. The reason why Madame Pernollet fell out of a window was never elucidated, and Gertrude Stein was deeply troubled by this mysterious death. She and Toklas had stayed at Madame Pernollet's hotel before they moved to Bilignin. Some people suggested that she was sleepwalking, others, including Stein, wondered if it was suicide.[4] The most disturbing feature of this affair was the unusually quick removal of the body because of the guests.

The second worrying event concerned Madame Caesar, a friend of Stein and Toklas, whose English friend was found dead with two bullets in her head after she had returned from a short visit in England. It was never discovered whether she had killed herself or whether a murder had been committed. During her absence, another friend of Madame Caesar, Madame Steiner, had moved in with Madame Caesar. Thus, there seem to have been intricate relationships between these women. Stein was obviously troubled by this obscure death as well; she had her doubts about the suicide version. In *Everybody's Autobiography* she deals with this event in great detail (*EA*, pp. 79–83).

Another, less tragic event was the servant problem: Stein and Toklas hired a couple in Lyon whom they sent away after strange things happened at their Bilignin home (their friend's car was tampered with, the telephone did not work).[5] In the middle of all this turmoil, Francis Rose, the painter, arrived with a friend, but Stein did not wish to see them because she had quarreled with them before, so she sent them away as well.

In *Blood on the Dining-Room Floor*, these incidents are presented as if they *were* all connected. The effect of this linkage enhances expectations that someone—the detective—can explain these links, and thus solve the mystery behind all these events. To find out what happened is one of the main characteristics of the detective novel, but also of Stein's writing projects in general. As already discussed, in *Four in America* the relationship between "what happens" and "what is" constitutes the starting point of her exploration of the four American heroes. She is particularly explicit in *Everybody's Autobiography* where she comments on Madame Steiner: "It never bothered us any more but every time I want to write I want to write about what happened to her" (*EA*, p. 83).[6] Furthermore, these events lend themselves especially well to an investigation of the question What happened? because they are all mysterious in some ways. But they are also connected with everyday life at home. Therefore, Ellen Berry speaks of "domestic tragedies"[7] that can indeed take place in the dining room: Commonness and mysteriousness are interrelated, and both need investigation. In her essay "Why I Like Detective Stories" Stein states that she "like[s] detecting" because "there are so many things to detect" and she gives examples from her own life (e.g., "why did somebody say what they said," or "why did somebody cut out a paragraph in the proof I was correcting").[8] At the same time, she emphasizes how well Edgar Wallace's detective stories are written because there is no detection in them, or, as she puts it, "he makes it ordinary."[9] Thus, it seems that for Stein, detection is attractive and fascinating, but it is also quite a natural, ordinary thing. For her, this relationship is not at all contradictory; it is part of her deep interest in human life with its usual commonplaces that are yet existential. Writing about these usual events in a form that enables the writer to explore them in a new way is the main goal of Stein's ambitious project. The detective story with detection at its core seems to have been a solution to overcome Stein's writing block because she had to describe events that needed investigation and detection. Moreover, she had always been an avid reader of detective stories and was a great admirer of the genre. However, her detective story does not conform to the main characteristics of the genre.

The most obvious feature of the detective novel is its hero, the detective whose goal is detection. "[T]he detective cannot be a fool,"[10] is a requisite that must be fulfilled at any rate. But Stein does away with the hero "as logical force"[11] and instead introduces a first-person narrator who seems to be the protagonist but is never really identified. He or she[12] has nothing in common with the detective hero typical of the genre since Edgar Allan Poe's "The Murders in the Rue Morgue" and "The Purloined Letter," the detective "who reconstructs the scene of a crime and apprehends the guilty party through the traces left behind."[13] Thus, Stein's detective novel has no city stroller, Walter Benjamin's *flâneur*,[14] another characteristic of the detective hero; instead, there is an unidentified narrator who is obsessed with the question What happened? Trying to *write* about what happened is much more important than finding out who has committed the crime(s). Indeed, the narrator again and again emphasizes that she tries very hard to write about these events: "Now I will try to tell" (p. 15). The numerous direct pleas to the reader similarly express the narrator's deep concern to describe what happened: "Listen to this one," "Do you really understand" (p. 16), and "Do you hear" (p. 30). The narrator's anxiety about writing seems to replace the detective hero's role of investigating a murder. Writing and detecting almost mean the same in Stein's detective novel. The motives of the events she tries to write about can only be detected if they are put into words.

Stein's insistence on writing in spite of her difficulties might be responsible for the narrator's highly personal and individualistic stance. Unlike Benjamin's argument that there is a tendency in detective fiction toward "erasure of individuality,"[15] Stein uses a first-person narrator who not only writes about her writing problems but also establishes a very intimate relationship with the reader, although at the beginning the narrator cannot be recognized as a first-person narrator, and personal pronouns without obvious referents create an anonymous atmosphere. The book opens with the sentence "They had a country house" (p. 11), and it is never stated to whom "they" exactly refers. But as soon as the narrator directly addresses the reader, she makes it quite clear that she is concerned about the reception of her words, and distance and anonymity disappear. Stein does not use first-person pronouns for persons who are obviously herself and Toklas; instead, she sticks to "some one" ("Then some one else went out" [p. 13]) or "they" ("they had a country house," [p. 11]), which refer to herself or to herself and Toklas. Through the reading of *Everybody's Autobiography*, in which she uses first-person pronouns, we are familiar with the events described here. The narrative stance in the detective story creates a certain distance between the narrator and the other characters, but the intimate tone between narrator and reader is not affected by this impersonalization.

A comparison of the events in *Blood on the Dining-Room Floor* with the ones in *Everybody's Autobiography* illustrates once again how Stein presents personal experiences as fiction. Since these events are connected with mysterious deaths, the transformation into fiction calls for particular attention. Moreover, we must take into consideration that Stein first wrote about these

deaths in this particular genre and only later told them in an explicitly autobiographical form (*Everybody's Autobiography* was begun in 1936).

   Blood on the Dining-Room Floor opens with the strange behavior of two servants working in a country house. Stein also mentions "two visitors, not young,
both women" (p. 13), who can be identified as Janet Scudder and a friend in
Everybody's Autobiography: "Janet Scudder announced that she was coming
with a friend" (*EA*, p. 60). But the two visitors could also refer to Madame
Caesar and her English friend who came to see Stein and Toklas the very same
day. It seems as if identification of the two women is deliberately complicated
or mystified. In the autobiography she mentions the departure of all four women
"then Janet and her friend left . . . and the other two the Frenchwoman and the
Englishwoman left" (*EA*, p. 62). Thus, writing about these events at least three
years later, Stein is more precise than in her detective novel—especially when it
comes to persons. We can even say that persons on the scene are generalized,
impersonalized, and made anonymous: "some one," "the owner of the car," "a
very sweet young man," "everybody went," "these," "a man and a wife," "she
[the wife] was dead," etc. Among the few Christian names that appear in the
whole book, "Lizzie" is the most eminent; this person only appears in the book
as the addressee of the narrator's pleading questions "Lizzie do you understand"
(p. 14) and "Lizzie do you mind" (p. 22), which also contribute to the above-
mentioned intimate relationship with the reader.[16]

   The impersonalization of persons and the narrator's personal tone are not
contradictory. On the one hand, Stein wants to write a detective novel in which
mysteries should be solved, on the other hand, her writing is an attempt at overcoming her creative block. Thus, the impersonal presentation of characters
enables her to create mysteriousness, but since the narrator herself is obsessed
with finding the truth, that is, writing about what happened, her personal
involvement is always audible. Indeed, statements such as "Now I will try to
tell" (p. 15), "I feel I do not know anything if I cry" (p. 25), "It is one way to try
to cry" (p. 38), and "Now can I think how I will try" (p. 50) can be read as hints
at Stein's enormous will to try to write. In her essay "Why I like Detective
Stories," which documents the writing of her detective novel, we come across
similar phrases such as "to try is to cry but I did try to write one [a detective
story]" (p. 148). In Stein's detective novel we witness the process of Stein's
writing, and we take part in the search for clues to the mysterious events.

   In spite of the fact that the book is more about the mystery of writing than
about the mystery of crime(s), crime and death occur. Franco Moretti suggests
that "[m]oney is always the motive of crime in detective fiction,"[17] and this rule
also applies to Stein's detective novel, although the connection between money
and crime is never made explicit. But in her essay on detective stories Stein ela-
borates on the issue of money, and she concludes that money is necessary for a
detective story. Unlike Moretti, who argues from a Marxist perspective that in
detective fiction people search for profit (through thefts, frauds, etc.) because of
the "unequal exchange between labour-power and wages,"[18] Stein describes the
crucial function of money with regard to crimes in her typically simplified but

very accurate way: "money is not money if you do not owe money to another."[19] Money is described as something that one must give to others (that is, when you owe somebody money); therefore, if one does not have to give money away, money is not an issue. In her short pieces on money—"Money," "More About Money," "All About Money," and "My Last About Money"[20]— she also explores the question of distribution of money between rich and poor people.

In *Blood on the Dining-Room Floor*, money is mentioned again and again, but never as a clear issue suggesting criminal actions. Being rich or poor is presented as an essential characteristic of people. Describing the owners of the hotel, the narrator points out that she "had come from poor people and he had not," and that in the meantime the family "grew richer and richer every day" (p. 19). These observations are of some significance with regard to the distribution of money in the family, but they can never really be recognized as causes or explanations for the mysterious events. Another family, the horticulturist family with their old mother, is similarly described: "Was she rich, were her sons rich, and were her daughters-in-law rich or had they ever been. Daughters-in-law can be rich, if they ever have been, rich" (p. 31). Although connections between the two families are suggested, detailed information is never supplied. Instead, the narrator summarizes her account like a teacher or, indeed, like a detective: "Has everybody got it straight. So far we have two families and besides a country house. We have three times crime" (p. 26), and the issue of money may be a link because of Madame Pernollet's money.

As money is mentioned repeatedly, so is crime, but only as a verbal icon. The speaker alludes to crime(s), but never explicitly describes one. She only knows that "[t]here are so many ways in which there is no crime" (p. 42). It seems that the borderline between crime and no crime is not distinguishable. The search to find out what happened may not lead to the exposure of any criminal actions at all, although the contrary is suggested at times. The question about the woman who fell to her death recurs repeatedly, but it remains unanswered till the very end. Detecting seems to be required, but it never happens. In "Why I Like Detective Stories," Stein comments on her detective novel, emphasizing that "nobody did any detecting except just conversation."[21] Thus, trying to write about what happened does not lead Stein to conclusions—only to new questions. Writing about detecting creates new issues that need to be written about again.

Writing about trying to write does not allow for character development; the only person who is not static is the narrator. In this respect, Stein's detective novel is "radically anti-novelistic," a characteristic of detective fiction, as Franco Moretti notes, because its characters "do not grow."[22] Moretti even claims that detective fiction's "object is to return to the beginning";[23] the detective story begins with the death of the individual and ends with the death of the criminal, or at least with the punishment of the criminal. Thus, the reader returns to the starting point, to the death of a person. At the end of Stein's detective story we also return to the beginning, but there is no criminal to be arrested and punished. The narrator's initial question "How did she die" (p. 15) is replaced by "Do you understand anything" (p. 81) at the end of the book, and the two concluding words form a question "Are they" (p. 81) referring to the preceding, ambiguous sentence "No one is amiss after servants are changed" (p. 81). Thus, the servant problem of the beginning concludes the book. Instead of a solution, detection, or punishment there are questions addressed to Lizzie, and/or to the reader. Teeming with questions, Stein's detective story leaves us with many possible answers; above all, the many recurring questions suggest multiple meanings.

Blood on the Dining-Room Floor can be described as a postmodern text "floating through textual space,"[24] as Ellen Berry points out, but similar to other Stein texts, it defies categorization and cannot only be called "a pastiche of detective conventions."[25] Of course, Stein's text does not meet a reader's expectations of a detective story, but neither is her text a parody of this genre. Stein chooses a particular genre because she considers it to be useful for her intentions, but then transforms it to fit her own needs and goals. Those, in turn, are intricately intertwined with Stein's daily life and struggle. In the case of *Blood on the Dining-Room Floor*, it is her writing block that is the core of her daily struggle, and together with the mysterious events of that summer, it becomes the material for a text that Stein labels detective fiction. Stein becomes her own detective, investigating her writing block, which can be called a crime for any writer. The genre as such is given by Stein herself, and we know that this labelling can never be trusted.

The genre of detective fiction undergoes a transformation in Stein's writing process that is marked by issues of gender in this book. The narrator's concern with female characters calls for particular attention. In the first place, the victim that preoccupies her is female, and her death seems to be connected with her husband's unfaithfulness ("he was unfaithful, and she knew that the night was a day," p. 20). The narrator's sympathies are quite obviously with the deluded woman. Her doubts about the version of the woman who walked in her sleep and then fell down are expressed again and again. She mistrusts Alexander the horticulturist who spread this rumor. The following passage is an example of the narrator's probing questions about the circumstances of the woman's death: "Did she walk in her sleep. Had she walked in her sleep. Who had walked in her sleep. Where did she walk. And whose was it that she walked. Whose was it. Can anybody cry" (p. 21). The insisting repetitions enhance the impression that the narrator might be thinking of a crime, although she never utters this suspicion explicitly. When she speaks to Lizzie directly, she conveys anxiety and concern for the dead woman, and also that Lizzie seems to mind ("Lizzie can it matter that you mind, if you mind it," p. 77). Thus, two female persons take sides with a third woman.

The presence and dominance of female characters are introduced at the very beginning of the detective story. The narrator mentions the two visitors at the country house; they are "not young, both women" (p. 13). Through the presence of female figures and through both the narrator's voice and the person she addresses, that is, Lizzie, female perception is pervasive. The crucial question of Stein's detective novel—What has happened?—is thus always related with female characters, above all with the death of a woman. The notion of the clever, goal-oriented male detective is undermined as the narrator-detective acknowledges the uncertainties of her search and consequently repeats her question(s). Moreover, the fact that the narrator wants to detect like any detective creates a bond between telling a story and trying to detect a crime. Her admonition "Remember I wish to tell you in every way what they [everybody] do not say" (p. 39) characterizes her as a writer/artist who knows more than others but who also faces great difficulties in telling/writing. Thus, the narrator incorporates both writer, artist, *and* detective who, in turn, also provides us with a strong focus on women in the story. The combination of these multiple positions also make for a multiple form of genre, that is, a detective novel that is not one and yet pretends to be one. The paradox of the genre definition in Stein's case is once more a given. Therefore, nothing can be found out in her detective novel except that detection is the writer's and reader's orientation. "Read while I write" (p. 77) is uttered by the narrator, and as readers, we are directly involved in the writing process. But the request may also allude to Alice B. Toklas, who is reading what has already been written while Gertrude Stein continues to write down her search for words. We know that this kind of collaborative enterprise was part of their daily life together.

It is not surprising, then, that Stein describes the detective novel as "the only really modern novel" because "you have so to speak got rid of the event before the book begins."[26] Since, according to Stein, event and character belong to the nineteenth century, the genre of the detective novel with the corpse ("the event") right at the beginning of the book seems to be a useful genre, but as with other prescriptive patterns, Stein transforms it to her own needs. Moreover, her transformation not only belongs to the twentieth century but was well ahead of her own time.

Stein's disregard for events is particularly noticed by the postmodern poet John Ashbery, who, like Stein, is more interested in "their way of happening."[27] In *Blood on the Dining-Room Floor*, Stein's attempt to write in this way about the events of the summer of 1933 results in writing about writing, because the mysterious events she originally wanted to write about could not be disentangled. Writing about writing ends with a passage that could appear in any other work of Stein's, be it play, novel, or poem; it is a meditation about rendering experience in writing. In Chapter 12 I illustrate that her *Stanzas in Meditation*, although considered to be "poetry," is a work that transgresses genre precisely because of this goal of unmediated rendering of experience. Moreover, as it is considered to be "the other autobiography," that is, the companion book to *The Autobiography of Alice B. Toklas*, the issue of genre is inevitably linked with gender because of the positing of the lesbian subject.

NOTES

1. First published in 1948, Pawlet, Vermont. Quotations in the text refer to the following edition: Gertrude Stein, *Blood on the Dining-Room Floor*, ed. by John Herbert Gill (Berkeley, CA: Creative Arts Book Company, 1982). "A Murder Mystery" follows the title on the cover page of this edition.

2. Gertrude Stein, *How Writing Is Written*, ed. Robert Bartlett Haas (Los Angeles: Black Sparrow Press, 1974), pp. 31–36.

3. It is interesting to note how critics comment on these; they seem to be mystified by so many disturbing events. Some only mention Mrs. Pernollet's tragic death and the mysterious death of the English woman. Others also refer to the strange servants of the Stein-Toklas household or to a man called Alexander, who was also connected with the hotel Pernollet. See, for example, Ellen Berry, *Curved Thought and Textual Wandering: Gertrude Stein's Postmodernism* (Ann Arbor, MI: University of Michigan Press, 1992), p. 147.

4. In *The Geographical History of America* Stein writes about the hotel keeper's wife, though giving her another name: "as she had become dead that is she had killed herself just as much to be dead as not," p. 35.

5. For more detailed information about the couple's strange behavior, see Diana Souhami, *Gertrude and Alice* (London: Pandora, 1991), p. 197.

6. The pronoun "her" could perhaps also refer to the English woman, but since the preceding paragraph concerns Madame Steiner, I assume that Stein means Madame Steiner.

7. Ellen Berry, *Curved Thought*, p. 148.

8. Stein, "Why I Like Detective Stories," p. 147.

9. Ibid., p. 148.

10. Jacques Barzun, "Detection and Literary Art," in *Detective Fiction: A Collection of Critical Essays*, ed. Robin W. Winks (Englewood Cliffs, NJ: Prentice-Hall, 1980), p. 153.

11. Berry, *Curved Thought*, p. 146.

12. In the following discussion I will use the female pronoun owing to Susan Sniader Lanser's explanation, quoted in footnote 11 of Chapter 1.

13. Tony Bennett in his introduction to Chapter 4, "Knowledge, Power, Ideology: Detective Fiction" in *Popular Fiction: Technology, Ideology, Production, Reading*, ed. Tony Bennett (London: Routledge, 1990), p. 212.

14. Ibid., pp. 213–15.

15. Ibid., p. 213.

16. "Lizzie" may also be a wordplay on "listen," which would underline the narrator's pleas to the reader.

17. Franco Moretti, "Clues," in Bennett, *Popular Fiction*, p. 243.

18. Ibid. Moretti emphasizes that detective fiction never comments on the reasons of this relationship.

19. Stein, "Why I Like Detective Stories," in *How Writing Is Written*, p. 146.

20. In *How Writing Is Written*, pp. 106–12.

21. Stein, *How Writing Is Written*, pp. 148–49.

22. Franco Moretti, "Clues," in Bennett, *Popular Fiction*, p. 241.

23. Ibid.

24. Ellen Berry, *Curved Thought*, p. 149.

25. Ibid.

26. Stein, "What Are Master-Pieces and Why Are There So Few of Them," p. 87.

27. John Ashbery, "The Impossible," in *Critical Essays on Gertrude Stein*, ed. Michael Hoffman, p. 105. "The Impossible" is a review of Stein's *Stanzas in Meditation*, which originally appeared in *Poetry* 90, no. 4 (July 1957): 250–54.

12

Stanzas in Meditation
or Meditation in Stanzas

A POET MEDITATES

John Ashbery's deep interest in and enthusiasm for *Stanzas in Meditation* is not unexpected, as he himself is a poet whose work is indeed a "poet's prose."[1] His comments on this work are most revealing with regard to genre. He links the statement about Stein's disinterest in events quoted in Chapter 11 with another, crucial observation about Stein's writing—namely her attempt at rendering experience in real life through a language that does not mediate experience but establishes an analogue of it. Ashbery considers Stein's *Stanzas in Meditation* and Henry James's *The Golden Bowl* as examples of this way of writing (about) experience:

Both *Stanzas in Meditation* and *The Golden Bowl* are ambitious attempts to transmit a completely new picture of reality, of that *real* reality of the poet which Antonin Artaud called *"une réalité dangereuse et typique."* If these works are highly complex and, for some, unreadable, it is not only because of the complicatedness of life, the subject, but also because they actually imitate its rhythm, its way of happening, in an attempt to draw our attention to another aspect of its true nature.[2]

Ashbery accurately describes Stein's project of transforming life's immediacy into writing, and he is well aware of her innovativeness and the resulting risks for the reader. In his review of *Stanzas in Meditation*, the following remark about its genre is striking. He states that "this poem . . . is always threatening to become a novel," and, again, he mentions James's late novels such as *The Golden Bowl* and *The Sacred Fount*, which, as he puts it, "strain . . . toward 'the condition of music,' of poetry."[3] He links the issue of genre with the issue of un-mediated experience, but without exploring this interrelatedness any further. However, I believe that his description of Stein's work as "threatening to become a novel" suggests that her "poem" is bound to transgress genre because it aspires to include all of reality, of a moment's way of happening. Generic traditions, boundaries, or restraints would be impediments for such an ambitious project. Ashbery's description of Stein's writing is even more telling when we take his own "meditative prose pieces"[4] into consideration, because they share a number of characteristics with Stein's texts. In *Poet's Prose*, an investigation of American prose poems,[5] Stephen Fredman focuses on Ashbery's (impossible) attempt at creating "total mimesis" and claims that specific features of Ashbery's own *Three Poems* include "flatness and sameness of tone in a *meditation*" and "the mysterious energy generated by the persistence and seeming monotony of incomprehension."[6] This description can equally be applied to various texts by Stein. Fredman, at this point, does not pursue the implications of genre further; instead, he turns to theoretical remarks about translation in order to gain insights into Ashbery's difficult way of writing. It is interesting to note that Stein also uses the process of translating to describe the two ways of writing (see Chapter 10 on *Four in America*).

Fredman uses Walter Benjamin's theoretical approach to translation because this approach emphasizes the radical difference between the original work and its translation. Benjamin differentiates between the goals of the two processes of creation and translation: A translation should reproduce the signification of an original work in a "pure language," but it does not contain the poet's intention, which "is spontaneous, primary, graphic," while "that of the translator is derivative, ultimate, ideational."[7] This is reminiscent of Stein's statement about her experience as a translator—"that words come out differently if there is no recognition as the words are forming because recognition had already taken place." In Fredman's view, Ashbery's work is more ideational than primary or graphic because he endeavors to describe "the experience of experience."[8]

I do not want to discuss Fredman's judgment of Ashbery here because I am primarily interested in his use of the analogy of translation that is also most revealing with regard to Stein's writing. Stein aspires to combine the two ways of writing, as she makes clear in her section on Henry James in *Four in America*. Trying to write about experience without mediation, Stein, like Ashbery, constantly draws our attention to language and to its dual nature, namely the "self ordering system and the pointing system,"[9] and she disregards its categories and classifications of genre because they always play a mediating role in writing.

Stanzas in Meditation, not coincidentally also called Meditation in Stanzas by Stein,[10] contains a generic label and a prosodic term, the former referring to prose, the latter to poetry. Stanzas can also be understood as Italian "stanzas" for rooms; thus, there is the association of a private realm in which one meditates. If we think of the pun "meditation/mediation" we may consider the stanzas as mediators. The reversal or interchangeability makes evident what Stein is going to demonstrate in the course of her meditations or stanzas: We can read the texts both ways, or, more precisely, it does not matter with which generic spectacles we approach the text, although poetic expectations are aroused because we immediately associate stanzas with the poetic. Meditation is not clearly definable and defined;[11] therefore I shall use it in a very broad sense like Fredman, who does not actually define it but speaks of "meditative prose" or "meditative pieces," meaning poetry of prose that is philosophical, private, and exploratory.

This blurring of prose and poetry was already observed by Wendell Wilcox in 1940: "[I]n her [Stein's] own mind the distinction [between prose and poetry] was lost, or, to speak more accurately, abandoned. In her work the two have become one."[12]

Stein's own comment on meditation in "Sentences and Paragraphs" expands the generic aspect; furthermore, it also contains a crucial reference to gender categories:

> Now make a sentence all alone.
> They remember a walk. They remember
> a part of it. Which they took with them.
> Now who eases a pleasure.
> I ought to be a very happy woman.
> Premeditated meditation concerns analysis.
> Now this is a sentence but it might not be.
> Premeditated. That is meditated before meditation.
> Meditation. Means reserved the right to meditate.
> Concerns. This cannot be a word in a sentence.
> Because it is not of use in itself.
> Analysis is a womanly word. It means that they
> discover there are laws.[13]

Stein dissects the sentence "Premeditated meditation concerns analysis" word by word, exploring it and meditating upon it. She actually demonstrates what a sentence is by "performing" this sentence; although the sentence is "about" meditation, it is itself a meditation: The first person speaker/writer meditates upon the question as to what a sentence is. Being concerned with categories—a sentence is a unit defined according to rules and systems—she uses the word "womanly" in order to describe the word "analysis," which, in turn, characterizes "premeditated meditation." "Womanly" is further linked with "laws," with rules and prescriptions. The referent of "they" is not quite clear, but as is often the case in Stein's texts,—especially in *Stanzas in Meditation*—it can include the speaker and the addressee, but it can refer to others as well. Analysis associated with the female realm is unusual because it is traditionally conceived of as a domain of male logical thinking, and it is typical of our concept of science to link analytical activity with laws. The inherent contradiction that results in attributing a female characteristic to analysis on the one hand challenges the traditional understanding of male analytical capability, and on the other questions the relationship between analysis and law. The sentence "It means that they discover there are laws" implies that only female analysis can detect the existence of laws, and "they" (whoever they are) discover laws that are different from laws discovered by male analysis. A different reading may allude to the patriarchal laws enforced upon women as to how to make a sentence. As Stein demonstrates how such a different, "womanly" meditation occurs, we as readers are challenged to read differently because we cannot apply our methods of analysis based on logic, coherence, reference, etc.[14] Meditation thus is a process for Stein to explore difference; *Stanzas in Meditation* is an exploration of difference, both in genre and gender.

I AND THEY AND SHE: THE SUBJECTS OF MEDITATION

Stein advises young writers to "write meditations, meditations are always interesting, neither character nor identity are necessary to him who meditates." Character and identity seem to be disturbing factors in Stein's exploration of reality through language, although identity is a dominant theme in her works. But it cannot be a fixed notion for the writer, as she has emphasized in her definition of a masterpiece, which is created by the human mind—and the human mind has no identity. Indeed, the speaker's use of the personal prounouns "I" and "they" without identifiable referents at the very beginning of *Stanzas in Meditation* undermines any notion of fixed referents—that is, persons in this case—and thus neither characters nor identities can be specified: "I caught a bird which made a ball / And they thought better of it."[15] "I," "they," and "she" are pronouns that dominate the stanzas. Biographical material can be used to speculate about possible referents, but despite the usefulness of this material, these pronouns have multiple referents and do not necessarily refer to persons or characters.[16] They may be persons, but we primarily encounter them as voices—and predominantly that of the first-person meditating speaker.

This first-person speaker is in a constant dialogue with another voice or other voices that in turn address a "you." Similar to Ashbery's "shifting of personal pronouns, so that any person (first, second, third; singular or plural) can be the 'subject' of the prose,"[17] Stein's voices simultaneously create intimacy and collectiveness. The former hints at a relationship of lovers that is secret and not easily accessible and understandable to others; the latter includes everybody—it is "commonplace," or ordinary, as I have described in my section on *Blood on the Dining-Room Floor*. This notion of the commonplace is articulated by Stein herself when she has Toklas comment in *The Autobiography of Alice B. Toklas* on her *Stanzas in Meditation*: "I am trying to be as commonplace as I can be, she used to say to me. And then sometimes a little worried, it is not too commonplace. The last thing that she had finished, Stanzas in Meditation, and which I am now typewriting, she considers her real achievement of the commonplace" (*ABT*, p. 225). Stein's use of the word "commonplace" has the connotation of "a natural phenomenon, a thing existent in itself" (*ABT*, p. 224); it is what the writer sees around her and then tries to transform into writing without changing its nature—without complicating it, conceptualizing it, or categorizing it. She usually tries to avoid abstract words or theoretical terms in order to concentrate on the thing itself. This attempt is difficult because Stein tries to use a language that is free of rigid concepts or of a clear frame of reference in order to concentrate on the thing itself. Meditating upon the commonplace means approaching what she sees as closely and personally as possible (intimacy), but at the same time it also means encompassing all possibilities (collectiveness) of writing about it. "I," "they," and "she" are all part of and have a part in this world around us. In the following quotation Stein uses the word "landscape" again, serving as an example of how everybody perceives one's surroundings differently: "A landscape is what when they that is I / See and look" (p. 124). Difference and sameness are crucial for them and the "I," the one who meditates—and mediates.

DIFFERENCE, ALIKE, AND I LIKE

The word "difference" appears again and again throughout the stanzas, but not as often as "alike," "I like," or "they like." Both "difference" and the combinations[18] and puns with "like" are connected, not only because of the pair of opposites "difference-alike" but because Stein establishes a relationship among these words by exploring the modifying capability of language. How can one transpose similar perceptions into language and still create the newness and singularity of each moment?

Both the notion of sexual difference as developed by Lacan and Derrida's concept of *différance* theoretically illuminate Stein's creative endeavor through language. According to Lacan, sexual difference depends on whether a subject does or does not possess the phallus. The acquisition of language occurs at the same time as the child enters the symbolic order, which coincides with the Oedipal phase, when the child becomes aware of his or her gender identity. Therefore, the phallus as "a *seeming* value" (not visible perception counts but its attributed meaning) becomes the privileged signifier in language.[19] The concept of *différance*, in contrast to sexual difference, opposes a binary system (male/female) and posits a sliding of language that only arbitrarily establishes reference and identity. Although Derrida's notion of *différance* ultimately wants to displace the form of identity itself, it has been contested by feminists, as it, too, is trapped by binary thinking. Jacqueline Rose perceives this contradiction in the following terms: "For the effect of this general dispersal of subjectivity into a writing process where narrative, naming and propriation are undone, is the constant identification of the woman with the underside of truth."[20] It is not the task of this study to enter the debate about Derrida's relation to feminism, nor do I think that it is possible to make a final statement about subjectivity and sexual/textual difference. I am interested in illuminating Stein's revolutionary investigation of sexual/textual difference before Derrida and Lacan had ever articulated their ideas. Indeed, Stein's critical and creative approach anticipates contemporary critical readings by feminists of these two influential thinkers.

Stein's exploration of difference in her stanzas encompasses several realms that are closely interrelated: it is the realm of the autobiographical, that is, herself, her sexual identity, "she" who can be Alice B. Toklas, "they" (the others, the audience of her work); the realm of language, that is, names, naming, speaking and listening; the realm of animated and inanimate objects such as birds, kites, butterflies, flowers, or potatoes, whose description is always about their difference. Examples in each of these realms show that their mere combination and interrelatedness is based on a notion of difference. Stein's sexuality and preference ("I like,") and textuality ("alike") posit a difference and sameness at the same time. But this difference and sameness is never based on a polarized system such as male/female or like/dislike; instead, it is subject to change according to the moment of writing: "The difference is spreading" (*Tender Buttons*, p. 461).

The speaker's relationship to the "she" of the stanzas is intimate and loving, but at times it also conveys disagreement and even aggressiveness. As there are several clearly recognizable biographical references to Alice B. Toklas, and as Stein's sexuality in the text is inseparable from Toklas's presence in the text, I shall read "she" as a referent to Toklas. The three stanzas V, VI, and VII of part 4, each of which consists of only one sentence, illustrate the speaker's own reference to sexuality and textuality: "I think very well of my way. / May be I do but I doubt it. / Can be can be men" (p. 71). The first statement is so ambiguous that it can of course refer to more than the speaker's sexual preference, that is, her lesbian identity and her "way" of writing; "my way" can encompass many different characteristics of the speaker. Yet, considering the other references to the speaker's relationship with "her" and to her position as a writer, "my way" appears less indefinite. The sentence that follows, directly related to the first, already calls into question in a typically Steinian way what the speaker has self-assertively articulated. Doubt, then, can refer to both the speaker's way of sexual preference and her way of being an artist.

The third sentence, "Can be can be men," explicitly designates the male sex, but the position of the predicate is not clear. "Men" can be read as an addition to "can be," which, in turn, picks up "May be" of the preceding line. This reading either suggests that it "can be" that "men" think well of the speaker's way, or that they (men) also express doubt about "[her] way." Thus, "men" is used as a contrast to position herself as woman, both in her sexuality and in the text. This gendered reading can be supported if we consider that Stein revised this text, and "[a]lmost consistently, the auxiliary verb *may* is changed to *can*."[21] According to Ulla Dydo, the reason behind these revisions was Stein's love affair with *May* Bookstaver, about which Stein writes in her early novel *Q.E.D.*, but whose manuscript Toklas only saw in 1932.

A passage with an obvious autobiographical reference to Toklas hints at their intimate daily relationship both in their love life as well as in their cooperation with regard to Stein's life as a writer. The beginning of the passage refers to an episode that is also related in *The Autobiography of Alice B. Toklas*: Toklas can recognize geniuses (see *ABT*, p. 5), and Stein is one of them. The autobiography gives us an ironized version because it is Toklas speaking through Stein, whereas in the stanzas Stein speaks directly to us:

She knew that she could know
That a genius was a genius
Because just so she could know
She did know three or so

So she says and what she says
No one can deny or try
What if she says.
Many can be unkind but welcome to be kind
Which they agree to agree to follow behind.
Her here. (p. 77)

"She" is described as a person indispensable to the speaker's life because she has both the intellectual capability to judge other people, relate to them ("welcome to be kind"), and make the speaker feel her omnipresence ("Her here"). The relationship between them is not hierarchical, even if the one, the writer, speaks for "her," and her presence is almost overwhelming. The crucial line in the same stanza, "She will be me when this you see," on the one hand comments on *The Autobiography of Alice B. Toklas*, in which the "she" is presented as the writer of her autobiography, and on the other hand acknowledges that the difference between "she" and "me" is no longer perceivable in writing ("when this you see"), although the difference between the two is always written about: "Two and one is two" (p. 75) and "Two think I think I think they will be too / Two and one make two for you" (p. 74).

Quite at the beginning the speaker even refers to the weight of the two and mentions a difference in this respect: "We two remember two two who are thin / Who are fat with glory too with two" (p. 9). Yet again the speaker includes "two" who are both thin and fat; thus, she does not distinguish between one (Toklas) who is thin and the other (Stein) who is heavy. This autobiographical reference to the prominent difference between Toklas's and Stein's weight illustrates the private realm of this "autobiography." Only readers familiar with this fact can recognize the speaker's concern about bodily difference and sameness.

An even more personal and intimate address to the (a) lover can be found in stanza IX of the third part: The speaker addresses her "darling" in words that are reminiscent of popular love songs or cliché-like expressions. But these words are extended to very unusual combinations and give evidence of Stein's playful and inquiring approach to language.

Tell me darling tell me true
Am I all the world to you
And the world of what does it consist
Can they be a chance to can they be desist
This come to a difference in confusion
Or do they measure this with resist with
Not more which.
Than a conclusion. (p. 50)

Only the first three lines seem to be compatible with correct English grammar whereas the other lines consist of elliptical phrases (e.g., "Can they be") or of incomplete sequences (e.g., "a chance to"), and they only make sense if we insert pauses. The "you" that is addressed at the beginning of this passage is embedded in a more coherent structure than the "they" that follows. The topic of the relationship between the speaker and her "darling" is expanded to a noncoherent description of the action of "they" ("they measure this"), which culminates in the word "conclusion." "Conclusion" interestingly enough rhymes with "confusion" of the preceding sentence, which undermines the connotation of "conclusion."

As mentioned above, the ubiquitous "they" have no clearly definable referents. But the numerous passages with "they" also contain the verb "to like," which implies that "they" react in a certain way to the speaker, and the speaker herself is concerned about this reaction. Although "they" sometimes includes the speaker, I shall focus on a passage that seems to proclaim "they" as an audience reacting:

> How often very often do they go
> Not which they wish or not which they wish
> However it is better not to like it at all
> I find it suddenly very warm and this can easily be
> Because after all may be it is
> In which case do they need any more explanation
> Or indeed will they bother
> Or after all can there be any difference
> Between once in a while and very often
> And not at all and why not and will they
> Should they be pleased with everything just the same
> So that they will think how well they like
> What they will do which they do
> For them at all.
> It is often no matter and a difference
> That they see this when they look here
> And they can very well be ready
> To see this when they look where they do
> Nor or can they be there where they are
> But not there where they are when
> They are at once pleased with what they have
> As they do not wish not only but also
> To have it better where they like. (pp. 32–33)

The speaker is anxious about "their" reaction ("will they bother") and tries to state reasons for or against certain preferences ("However it is better"; "Or after all can there be any difference"). These statements lead to a question such as "can they be there where they are," which seems to be a paradoxical sentence because the speaker assumes a place ("there") where "they" are and yet questions their whereabouts all the same. The speaker constantly and insistently explores "their" reactions and/or actions by stating the possibilities they have at hand (e.g., "Should they be pleased with everything just the same" and "They are at once pleased with what they have"). The different possibilities all turn out to be very much alike.[22] Difference explored in naming and names includes the speaker's "I," as it is her project of articulating difference through writing. The following stanza provides a subtle, precise and at the same time playful, artistic approach to the options language offers when challenged in this way:

What I wish to say is this of course
It is the same of course
Not yet of course
But which they will not only yet
Of course.
This brings me back to this of course.
It is the same of course it is the same
Now even not the name
But which is it when they gathered which
A broad black butterfly is white with this.
Which is which which of course
Did which of course
Why I wish to say in reason is this.
When they begin I did begin and win
Win which of course.
It is easy to say easily.
That this is the same in which I do not do not like the name
Which wind of course.
This which I say is this
Which it is.
It is a difference in which I send alike
In which instance which.

. . .

Now there is an interference in this.
I interfere in I interfere in which this.
They do not count alike.
One two three. (pp. 125–26)

The speaker minutely describes the tranformation between the thing observed and the thing named. She uses the phrase "of course" in order to express the commonness of a statement, but as she uses it she becomes aware of the many implications of "of course." The word "which" is also repeated to demonstrate its multiple referents within one sentence. The speaker investigates the problem of referentiality in language and comes to the conclusion that it has no limits, no borders. In a preceding stanza she illustrates what Saussure calls the minimal pair of phonemes necessary for difference: "Can you question the difference between lend. / Or not lend / Or not send / Or not leant" (p. 70). Now her attempt at pinning down the endless play between signifier and signified becomes an interchange of difference and sameness that originates in the speaker: "It is a difference in which *I* send alike." Whatever she wants to say, it is alike to what has been said before, and yet, the articulation of this very same is interfered with by the "I" and thus creates difference. The pun "I"/"eye" previously referred to points to the act of seeing as an additional "disturbing" factor in the process of naming: the discrepancy between what the eye sees and what language produces. The second pun "alike"/"I like" and, we may add, "Alice," ingeniously expresses the speaker's love for words that are always referring back to other, similar and different words, all of which she likes. The reading "It is a difference in which I send Alice"[23] tells us about the speaker's interrelatedness with Alice in every action, above all in using words, in language. The sexual difference alluded to is based on sameness of the two female figures, not on difference.

The fourth realm of difference, that of objects, is like a structuralist linguistic course on meaning. The speaker questions the reasons behind the attribution of a certain linguistic sign to an object: "They call peas beans and raspberries strawberries or two / They forget well and change it as a last" (p. 9). Another example taken from the stanza quoted above is striking, as it is often used as a literary symbol and does not belong to the commonplace of Stein's world, and yet it is something everybody knows and also sees: "But which is it when they gathered which / A broad black butterfly is white with this." Stein seems to imply that language expressing the poetic is always different according to the one re-creating it, and therefore we cannot take for granted a broad black butterfly because it could well be white. Black and white, we might say, are very much alike, in spite of their difference.

Stein's meditation about difference leads us through many stanzas (the work is more than 150 pages long), and at the end the speaker finally acknowledges that "[t]hese stanzas are done" (p. 151), although she repeats her doubts: "I am trying to say something but I have not said it. / Why. / Because I add my my I" (p. 126). Difference is located within herself and is subject to constant change and addition. But she assures us of her inclination for liking: "I like that I like" (p. 147), or "I like what I like" (p. 135). Pleasure in liking takes place in the attempt at unmediated rendering of experience, which in Stein's case always includes her companion Toklas ("Everybody knows that I chose," p. 151). Therefore, *Stanzas in Meditation* can be called autobiography, but as it is also a philosophical meditation on difference and likeness including gender difference in stanzas, that is, in a poetic form, it is not possible to attribute it to any one genre. To classify a text that explores difference and sameness through writing and sexual preference would deny what the text wants to challenge. In Stein's text neither genre nor gender difference can be classified because Stein constantly creates new difference and likeness: Her writing "ex-creates" classification.

NOTES

1. Stephen Fredman, *Poet's Prose: The Crisis in American Verse* (Cambridge: Cambridge University Press, 1983).

2. John Ashbery, "The Impossible," in *Critical Essays on Gertrude Stein*, ed. Michael Hoffman (Boston: G. K. Hall, 1986), p. 106.

3. Ibid., p. 105.

4. Fredman, *Poet's Prose*, p. 99.

5. Fredman's explanation of the term "poet's prose" instead of prose poem is convincing: "'Poet's Prose' . . . is proposed as a more encompassing term to cover all (not only lyric) poetry written in sentences rather than verse. The term is descriptive instead of normative; it applies to works that are conceived of and read as extensions of poetry rather than as contributions to one of the existing prose genres," ibid., p. vii.

6. Ibid., p. 101, my emphasis.

7. Walter Benjamin, *Illuminations*, ed. Hannah Arendt, trans. Harry Zohn (New York: Harcourt Brace & World, 1968), pp. 76–77. Quoted in Fredman, *Poet's Prose*, p. 104.

8. Ibid., p. 104.

9. David Antin, "Some Questions about Modernism," *Occident*, n.s. 8 (Spring 1974): 13. Quoted by Fredman, p. 140. This essay is also reprinted, in an abridged form, in Richard Kostelanetz's anthology *Gertrude Stein Advanced: An Anthology of Criticism*, pp. 208–12.

10. See Ulla Dydo, "Gertrude Stein: Composition as Meditation," in *Gertrude Stein and The Making of Literature*, ed. Neuman and Nadel, p. 45. In Dydo's recent *A Stein Reader*, Dydo also mentions this fact but uses the plural: "Meditations in Stanzas," Dydo, p. 468. As she does not give a reference, I do not know whether this is only a printer's error.

11. I consulted various dictionaries of literary terms and was surprised that "meditation" was not listed. Meditation, of course, also has the religious connotation that emphasizes the *experience* of meditating, that is, the spiritual exercise of exploring one's self in a divine presence. It is probably not a coincidence that Stein was fascinated by St. Teresa whose religious meditations she had read. See the appendix for a brief discussion of St. Teresa in connection with Stein's opera *Four Saints in Three Acts*. Richard Bridgman quotes Stein from an interview in which she said that she had "read the meditations of St. Therese whose mysticism was 'real and practical'" (*New York Times*, 17 November 1934, 13), in Bridgman, *Gertrude Stein in Pieces*, p. 178n.

12. Wendell Wilcox, "A Note on Stein and Abstraction," in *Gertrude Stein Advanced*, ed. Kostelanetz, p. 105. It originally appeared in *Poetry* (1940).

13. Stein, *How to Write*, pp. 31–32.

14. Ulla Dydo gives a different reading of this passage; in fact, she states that Stein's explanation of the sentence "is emptily methodical." "Gertrude Stein: Composition as Meditation," p. 48.

15. Stein, *Stanzas in Meditation*, p. 3. Although *Stanzas in Meditation* is part of the posthumous book called *Stanzas in Meditation and Other Poems [1929–1933]* (New Haven, CT: Yale University Press, 1956), most critics, myself included, agree on the fact that it is a work in its own. All further page references are from this edition.

16. Richard Bridgman also mentions these three pronouns, but he assumes that they are "three main characters." *Gertrude Stein in Pieces*, p. 214. See also Neil Schmitz, "The Difference of Her Likeness: Gertrude Stein's *Stanzas in Meditation*," in *Gertrude Stein and the Making of Literature*, ed. Neuman and Nadel, especially pp. 133–36. Schmitz convincingly argues that the pronouns cannot be attributed to specific persons or characters because of "the anonymous personality of the pronoun that suits Gertrude Stein," p. 135.

17. Fredman, *Poet's Prose*, p. 114. Ashbery himself also gives an illuminating comment on this multivocal use of pronouns. See Fredman, p. 114.

18. I intentionally use the word combination because it applies well to Stein's use of the word "like" with other words. Grammatical terms like pronoun-verb or adverb do not adequately describe the meaning of Stein's use of "like."

19. For a more detailed and precise overview of Lacan's notion of sexual difference viewed from a feminist position, see Rose, *Sexuality in the Field of Vision*, pp. 60–68. Rose uses the phrase "a *seeming* value," p. 66.

20. Ibid., p. 21.

21. Dydo, in her introduction to the extracts from *Stanzas in Meditation*, in *A Stein Reader*, p. 568.

22. For a different but nevertheless very convincing interpretation of "they," see Schmitz, "The Difference of Her Likeness," in *Gertrude Stein and the Making of Literature*, ed. Shirley Neuman and Ira B. Nadel (London: Macmillan, 1988), p. 142. He relies on Stein's phrase "'they' that is I" and concludes that "'they' represent representing."

23. Schmitz also refers to this pun and emphasizes that in Stein's text there is "the continual inscription of the beloved, tribute and testimony." See Schmitz, "The Difference of Her Likeness," p. 140.

V

Conclusion

13

Conclusion

At the beginning of this study I argued that Gertrude Stein deconstructs genre and that this deconstruction is related to the ways gender appears in her texts. In the course of investigating this process I have become increasingly suspicious of my own methodological apparatus. Although I believe that I was able to pinpoint crucial characteristics of Stein's approach to genre and to the role gender plays in this enterprise, I had to grapple with the inadequacy of a critic's language vis-à-vis Stein's use of language—a critic's language that relies on theoretical concepts that are meant to uncover patterns and systems in a writer's work, whose language undermines the very notion of their logic. Therefore, writing a conclusion at the end of a study on Stein feels like a highly contradictory act. Yet, as I have come to temporary conclusions after each part of the book, I shall aim at restating and connecting them in a way that does not dispense with the genre of literary theoretical discourse—be it only to prove that undermining the genre generates new forms of conclusion.

In Part 1 I dealt with two works from very different periods in Stein's life. Both implicitly (*The Making of Americans: Being a History of a Family's Progress*) and explicitly (*Ida A Novel*) use the generic label "novel," and both deconstruct the genre radically. In each of the two works the issue of gender plays a unique role in the deconstruction of the genre. In *The Making of Americans* the female narrator disappears, and an unidentified voice speaks of impersonal subjects ("one," "any one," etc.) who replace the family and its members. The history of a family's progress that the first-person narrator has set out to tell us disintegrates into descriptions of unsexed and unidentified persons. The family dissolves, and the narrator, who has again and again expressed her personal relationship with her characters, no longer seems to care. I argue from a psychoanalytical perspective that Stein's history of a family had to break apart, considering her position as a lesbian writer. The intention to write about a family includes her attempt to describe the very many different traits of both women and men, beginning with the members of one American family. Yet, sexual difference does not turn out to be the basis for well-defined characteristics; on the contrary, Stein's use of "the bottom nature" of people suggests a refusal of clearly defined sexual categories.

The deconstruction of the patriarchal family goes hand in hand with the deconstruction of the novel depicting family histories. Only if gender and genre are considered together do we become aware of their intersections and the resulting tensions deriving from such concepts. Stein's early work *The Making of Americans* abolishes the family and patrilinearity, but gender persists and is responsible for new forms.

Ida A Novel, written some thirty years after *The Making of Americans*, challenges genre and gender in a different way. Similar to Stein's family history, *Ida A Novel* neither follows a linear narrative nor does it have fixed character descriptions. But whereas in the early work the construction of a textual subject was inconceivable because the family had to be deconstructed first, in the later work we witness the birth of Ida both as character and text. These are inseparable and therefore more than one; neither character nor book are determined by measurable units such as time or space. Character and book form an "entity text," a masterpiece that, according to Stein, belongs to the present without beginning or end. Phrases such as "No and yes" or "[i]f she goes out she comes in" (p. 154) represent the openness of this entity text; it is so undetermined that generic speculation becomes futile.

Stein's preference for what she calls plays, which significantly she also calls landscapes, has to do with her distrust of narrative. Thus, her early plays "tell what happened without telling stories" (*LA*, p. 122) in order to present a moment in the present without looking back or ahead. Immediacy is created through multiple pieces of dialogue. In both *A Circular Play* and *Ladies' Voices*, dialogues take place between unidentified persons, and yet, the specific linguistic code used between certain speakers hints at an intimate love relationship between women. But Stein's dialogic language never establishes a fixed position for a particular speaker; therefore the words uttered by the speakers somehow float without ever being attributed to a fixed person. Nevertheless, through the lesbian subject the speakers become gendered: they have "ladies' voices."

In this verbal and erotic play of and between words and speakers who are not identified, the generic label "play" no longer fulfills its function: Identifiable dramatis personae and/or plot, the two main features that constitute a play, are not present; instead, the indeterminacy of language creates a nonhierarchical, continuing play of meaning(s) that transcends the generic meaning of "play."

The opera *The Mother of Us All*, with the suffragist Susan B. Anthony as its protagonist, follows no structural pattern such as a chronology of acts or plot development. But unlike the other two plays, the characters can be identified, and even the fictional ones that cannot be associated with historical figures are recognizable by their names and their speeches. The deconstruction of the genre *opera* is linked with the deconstruction of male discourse exemplified by patriarchal figures such as Daniel Webster. Susan B. Anthony's dialogic language challenges male discourse, which is monologic throughout the play. But the periods of silence at the end hint at the limits to her use of language. It is finally not Susan B. Anthony as character who uncovers the patriarchal forms of voting (excluding the women and the African Americans at her time) but Stein's *composition* marked as an opera with a suffragist in its leading role. Undermining the genre and presenting the disembodied voice of one of the most prominent suffragists at the end indicate the search for a language that might transcend both genre and gender.

Among Stein's autobiographies, *The Autobiography of Alice B. Toklas* occupies a special place because it was intentionally written for a public that did not seem to approve of or understand Stein's more hermetic and difficult works. Therefore her ingenious use of Alice B. Toklas's autobiographical "I" enabled her to present herself as a "male" genius with Toklas in the role of housewife and typist. Speaking in the voice of somebody else, Stein can manipulate her self-presentation and evade confidential matters if necessary. This strategy is manifest in the way her relationship to Toklas is presented as a heterosexual arrangement, and thus cannot harm her reputation as a public figure. Making Toklas tell stories about Parisian celebrities of their literary salon instead of writing her (Stein's) "self," she questions the assumption that one can write one's self. Instead, Stein demonstrates that as a writer she is always in a continuing dialogue with another "I" because writing one's self includes "the other," be it lover, reader, the public, or the text written.

Everybody's Autobiography continues Stein's critical investigation of how to write about the self. The title refers to the paradox Stein tries to come to terms with: the *auto* (same, self) implies *some*body specific and therefore cannot be written by *everybody*. But as Stein's writing project of the self includes the other and others, the paradox of everybody's autobiography makes sense and undermines the notion of a fixed, centered self. Furthermore, Stein's explicit criticism of the patriarchal system ("fathering") is part of this autobiographical enterprise because she ignores its chronology, that is, its generational pattern. Neither Stein's nor *Everybody's Autobiography* can be recognized as such; only Stein as writer and woman writing against "the fathers" can be identified.

Wars I Have Seen, Stein's account of her and Toklas's life during World War II, also includes everybody's life (lives), as Stein's daily experiences in occupied France always relate to other people, to the people of her village or to her many Parisian friends. Events in other people's lives are described in as much detail as her own daily errands. Autobiography and biography merge, and Stein's self is present in both but not definable in either. Moreover, the numerous philosophical meditations on childhood, wars, or death are part of daily life; domestic affairs and philosophical thinking are not separate activities. Autobiography, biography, and meditation merge.

Four in America illustrates best how Stein's exploration of other people's lives not only includes her own life but also describes the problems of her literary creativity. Therefore, the lives of the four American heroes are changed and transformed to something much beyond biographical—and also autobiographical—representation. What we witness is Stein's unique attempt at writing herself into the landscape of American patriarchal (literary) history; her disregard for traditional forms, such as genres and notions of chronology or hierarchy, position her outside of this country called America; she is an exile "ex-creating" American writing.

Part 4, it seems, deals with two very different books—one a detective story and the other a poetic work—but considering the tentative conclusions from the preceding parts this generic "mixture" makes sense both for Stein's works and for the goal of my study.

Stein calls *Blood on the Dining-Room Floor* a detective story, but there is no detective to solve the mystery of the strange events the narrator describes. Instead, the narrator is immersed in her anxious search for making herself understood. Although the mystery about the hotel owner's death calls for detection, detection itself becomes the topic of the book and triggers the narrator's numerous questions. Only writing about the difficulties of writing can the narrator come to terms with the woman's violent death. Thus, the initial wish to find out *what* happened turns into a meditation on *how* things can be described. But this meditation does not provide answers because the process of rendering experience into writing needs to be investigated continuously.

The borderline between narrator and writer is extremely thin in this meditation on writing. Therefore, I have assumed a female narrator, who takes the place of the traditional male detective-hero. Thus, Stein's transformation of the detective story into a sort of detecting meditation about writing also creates a new detective figure: the woman writer in disguise. Even if a reader does not know about Stein's writing block at the time of the book's composition, he or she is made very aware of the writer's anxiety about creativity.

Stein's meditating about writing culminates in *Stanzas in Meditation*, although this has been considered a companion work to *The Autobiography of Alice B. Toklas*. But the very fact that it also deals with her relationship to Toklas and yet is a poetic exploration about unmediated rendering of experience makes it impossible to distinguish between autobiography and poem(s), or prose and poetry. Stein tries to express life in the least mediated way and thereby writes her (daily) life with Toklas into text. This process makes her invent a language that evades structures such as coherence, order, or hierarchy, which are imposed (secondary) systems. Her language is highly private and coded on the one hand, reflecting a (hidden) lesbian relationship, and simple, repetitive, common, and rhythmic on the other hand. Language is reduced to certain basic elements and, simultaneously, constructed/composed again. This de/construction is based on a search for difference in both life and language. The result is a constant shifting between sameness and difference; similar texts create new differences. In *Composition as Explanation*, Stein decribes this dynamic:

There is singularly nothing that makes a difference a difference in beginning and in the middle and in ending except that each generation has something different at which they are all looking. By this I mean so simply that anybody knows it that composition is the difference which makes each and all of them then different from other generations and this is what makes everything different otherwise they are all alike and everybody knows it because everybody says it.[1]

It is not surprising, then, that Stein's composition of difference includes herself, and a line between life and text cannot be drawn. Therefore it is impossible to classify her texts according to genres because any classification fixes her text and thus denies the existence of difference within that very text. And in Stein's case it would also mean denying the writer's claim for difference as far as homosexuality[2] is concerned. Stein's works demonstrate an "ultimate abolition of genres,"[3] but although I have given a gendered reading, the question remains whether we can also speak of an abolition of gender(s).

NOTES

1. Stein, *Selected Writings of Gertrude Stein*, ed. Carl Van Vechten (New York: Random House, 1962), p. 513.

2. Judith Butler points out that we need to theorize this difference: "The vocabulary for describing the difficult play, crossing and destabilization of masculine and feminine identifications within homosexuality has only begun to emerge within theoretical language: the non-academic language historically embedded in gay communities is here much more instructive. The thought of sexual difference *within* homosexuality has yet to be theorized in its complexity." *Bodies That Matter: On the Discursive Limits of "Sex,"* (New York: Routledge, 1993), pp. 239–40.

3. Octavio Paz, *Children of the Mire: Modern Poetry from Romanticism to the Avant-Garde*, trans. Rachel Phillips (Cambridge, MA: Harvard University Press, 1974), p. 159.

VI

Stein's Compositional
Approach:
Beginning and Beginning

14

Composing and Rearranging

It is uncommon to continue after a conclusion, but because I have tried to illustrate that we must move away from sequential thinking with regard to Stein's works, I decided to "conclude" with a kind of beginning, namely with a children's book by Stein. One of the main themes of this children's book is the roundness of our world: It has neither a beginning nor an end. But the circularity implies the beginning of a new life—of a child. For Stein, writing life into text means beginning again and again.

Most of the texts analyzed in this study have appeared in different forms at different times in her literary career, with different generic labels. I have shown how Stein used material again and again, modifying and changing it according to a logic or plan that remains hidden from us. Yet, as I have argued, I believe that Stein worked with her material in a way that generated new meanings through the process of rearranging, or, as she called it, composing.

In this section I want to try to show—to a certain extent—why and how Stein rearranged material. In the appendix I shall focus on some of Stein's manuscripts because she not only inserted parts of her notes into later texts, with more or less obvious modifications, but also used certain notes in very different texts—and genres.

I also chose Stein's only children's book, *The World Is Round*, because Stein wrote it for a child she knew, and thus, for once, the generic label, is adequate as far as its recipient is concerned.[1] Yet, as we have observed in the previous chapters, material in this children's book also occurs in other texts—or genres.

In her *Composition as Explanation*, Stein emphasizes that "[e]verything is the same except composition and as the composition is different and always going to be different everything is not the same."[2] Her explanation is based on her concept of resemblance and difference, elaborated in the last chapter, but here again she makes clear that *everything* that reappears is already something else. The process of change is initiated by the artist who then becomes the "composer" of something new, something different. Stein's writing thus always refers back to something already written, heard, or spoken, but it also points toward the next composition. This process can be called circular in the sense that it goes forward even as it turns backward. Only the form of the circle encompasses a forward *and* backward movement that is dynamic and never-ending.[3]

NOTES

1. The various attempts to define children's literature show that it is almost impossible to stick to one particular definition; therefore, I shall follow Peter Hunt's convincing suggestion. Hunt focuses on the implied reader and concludes after a detailed discussion of various definitions by critics "that a particular . . . was written expressly for children who are recognizably children, with a childhood recognizable today, must be part of the definition" (Hunt, *Criticism, Theory, and Children's Literature* [Oxford: Basil Blackwell, 1991], p. 62).

2. Stein, "Composition as Explanation," in *Selected Writings by Gertrude Stein*, p. 516.

3. In Chapter 3 on Stein's "A Circular Play," I have commented on other characteristics of the circle, such as nonlinearity.

15

Rose and (Her) Autobiography

Stein wrote *The World Is Round* for the daughter of a close friend, Baroness d'Aiguy, called Rose Lucy Renée Anne.[1] But the name Rose[2] had already been crucial to her ideas and previous texts. First I want to consider a short text that is obviously a close companion to the children's book, one Stein wrote in 1936 entitled "The Autobiography of Rose."[3] The label "autobiography" is not surprising because, as I have shown in Part 3 on "autobiographies," for Stein, writing is a process of writing *life*, hers and the lives of "everybody." Indeed, Stein even incorporates her own name in the very last sentence of "The Autobiography of Rose": "Which is a pleasure to her friend, Gertrude Stein" (p. 42). Rose, the subject of the autobiography, is closely associated with the author of Rose's autobiography, again a narrative device to deconstruct the notion of an independent and autonomous autobiographical self.

The short text begins with the narrator's question about the reliability of a name. As in *Four in America,* Stein questions the relation between name and person, that is, What kind of an autobiography would Rose have if her name were not Rose? This seemingly paradoxical question addresses the issue of identity in a direct and also rather childlike manner: "And if her name is not Rose what would be her autobiography. It would not be the autobiography of Rose because her name would not be Rose. But it is the autobiography of Rose even if her name is not Rose oh yes indeed it is the autobiography of Rose" (p. 39). Children usually associate very definite characteristics with a particular name because they always relate a name with a person they know—and like or dislike. For them, a personal name has an identity as if it represented the person. While this process is very spontaneous and irrational, it also illustrates that words are never isolated from a cultural and social context. Stein, as an adult and a writer, expresses this phenomenon in her text by relying on the emotional approach of a child, and yet creates a linguistic sequence that becomes an artistic expression of language.

Stein's insistence on the relationship between name and autobiography at the beginning of this short piece is once again an investigation of identity. She deconstructs the autobiography genre by ignoring the autobiographical subject (we never hear Rose use the first person; instead there is a third-person narrator) and by using the title "The Autobiography of Rose" as subtitles for nine paragraphs. A few of these paragraphs are set apart from the rest of the text and consist of short lines—as if meant to be read as poems—as in the following:

> Is it taller to be taller.
> Is it older to be older.
> Is it younger to be younger.
> Is it older to be older.
> Is it taller to be taller. (p. 40)

The preceding line "Rose is her name that is what she said" (p. 40) introduces this poem. Reading an autobiography (of Rose) with such a tag line "she said," the reader is once again made aware that there is another voice telling the story and that Rose only has a voice through another. The recurring considerations about the personal name Rose enhance the challenging attitude toward this autobiographical self, supposedly a girl called Rose.

Rose is a seven-year-old girl, a statement made by the narrative voice, the biographer as it were, and we begin to wonder what possible contents the autobiography of a seven-year-old might have. It seems as if the title *The Autobiography of Rose* is a joke, for both the reader and the narrator. Yet, this text does not abound with humor. This short "autobiography" is about growing up, finding one's way in the world, and becoming aware of time and space. (This is also one of the main themes of *The World Is Round*.) Growing up for a girl means being confronted with all kinds of experiences, among them, recognizing that there are two (biological) sexes, namely "there is a little boy" and "there is a little girl," "his name is Allan," "her name is Rose" (p. 39). But this second paragraph (titled "The Autobiography of Rose") mentions not only the male and female sex but also crucial events and differences in life and nature such as the changing seasons ("There there is sunshine / Here there is snow," p. 39) and transformations achieved by human beings ("Grass that is cut is hay," p. 39).

These descriptions are introduced by two illuminating sentences: "Rose knew about afraid and when it happened she knew about afraid. This is what happened" (p. 39). Although the grammmatical sentence "Rose knew about afraid" can be read as "Rose knew and she was afraid" or "Rose knew about what it meant to be afraid," both readings allude to a kind of initiation that is fearful to a child—or girl. Thus, although Rose is only seven years old, she can already relate a (life) story about her experiences. Indeed, even Rose's seven years of life are quite a period when we consider together with Stein "How young do you have to be to be young. . . . Seven is not old for Rose but is it young" (p. 41).

These questions finally lead to the philosophical observation that time and one's age are always relative; when Rose was younger, she was certainly young, but now she is also young. Together with the age question we are made aware of the writer's time: "And now. Every time is every time. And Rose is young. . . . Has she an autobiography of when she was young" (p. 41). The fusion of the past (when Rose was young) and the present (Has she now an autobiography?) provide evidence of the problematic attitude of a writer toward his/her own life that is written about. Stein not only challenges the autobiographical approach by writing an autobiography of a seven-year-old but also deeply questions the notion that a certain age and a special life are necessary to acquire a knowledge worthwhile to be narrated.

"The Autobiography of Rose" not only contains essential observations that are taken up again in *The World Is Round* but also is an introduction to a girl's growing up and at the same time a reflection of what one writes when growing up. Stein's ending playfully conveys to us that even Gertrude Stein as a writer can write an autobiography of a seven-year-old, but that we must never believe that it is the only one:

THE AUTOBIOGRAPHY OF ROSE.
Rose. What can she remember. Can she remember Rose. Can she. I am wondering.

To Rose. *When they said if she would be good, she said she would know all about it all the same, and all the same she can know all about it. Which is a pleasure to her friend,* Gertrude Stein. (p. 42)

The writer Stein explicitly inscribes her own name into Rose's autobiography and states her own pleasure. It remains open whether pleasure refers to writing with/for Rose, or whether it is evoked because of Rose's knowledge ("she can know all about it"). In any case, it gives evidence of the *jouissance* we have previously found in Stein's language.

"The Autobiography of Rose" is one of the many autobiographies Stein wrote, and I do not think that "[b]y itself it resists interpretation."[4] Considering it as a companion text to *The World Is Round*, the question arises whether Stein had already thought of Rose d'Aiguy, the girl to whom she dedicated the latter book, when writing this autobiography. I argue that since the issue of identity is at the core of both an autobiography and a children's book, Stein did not want to distinguish between these two texts. A children's book is not necessarily an autobiography of a child, but it deals with aspects concerning a child's identity, be it indirectly through a plot or more explicitly through the narration of a child's life, an animal's life, or the life of another (human) being.

NOTES

1. See Stein, *The World Is Round* (London: William Clows and Sons, 1939), p. 4. Further references to this edition are given in the text. See also Bridgman, *Gertrude Stein in Pieces* (New York: Oxford University Press, 1970), p. 299, for the publication history. The Baroness translated Stein's *Paris France* into French.

2. Besides the name Rose, Stein also used the noun "rose" to elucidate her views on poetry. See the now famous sequence "A rose is a rose is a rose is a rose," *Lectures in America*, p. 231. In her essay on "Chiens et Maris dans Ida," Florence Delay comments on a possible French and English reading: "Rose is arose is arose is arose," meaning the French "arroser" besides the English verb "arise" (Delay, *in'hui: Gertrude Stein, Encore*, no. 0 [1983]: p. 83). The first instance occurs in "Sacred Emily," in *Geography & Plays*, p. 187. In her essay "The Revolutionary Power of a Woman's Laughter," Jo-Anne Isaak mentions Marcel Duchamp's famous "Rrose Sélavy" (Eros, c'est la vie) together with Stein's rose poem. Moreover, Isaak relates Stein's rose poem to a contemporary artist's "plastic poem" about rose/eros. See *Gertrude Stein Advanced*, ed. Richard Kostelanetz, p. 35.

3. In *How Writing Is Written*, ed. Robert Haas (Los Angeles: Black Sparrow Press, 1974), pp. 39–42.

4. Bridgman, *Gertrude Stein in Pieces*, p. 299.

16

The Round World of Rose and Rose and Rose and Rose

Stein's only children's book may be regarded as a personal dedication to a friend's little daughter, but it can also be considered as a logical development of Stein's deconstruction of genres: Writing texts that constantly exlore the process of writing and the process of living, she cannot but create a book for a child that equally explores (her-)self and the child—or children at large. Here I shall discuss the reasons why the round world of Rose is connected with the search for identity and for writing.

The World Is Round begins like most children's books, namely with the famous phrase "[o]nce upon a time" (p. 5). Stein seems to deliberately use the conventional opening of a story for children in order to create an atmosphere in which children will recognize certain structures in both story and discourse. But the well-known phrase does not continue with "there was a"; instead it runs: "once upon a time the world was round" (p. 5), a rather theoretical statement for children. Nevertheless, the second paragraph continues with the more familiar mode, mentioning all kinds of animals besides men and women before introducing Rose. A children's world is created, but at the same time there are statements that provoke questions also aimed at adults: "Rose was her name and would she have been Rose if her name had not been Rose. She used to think and then she used to think again" (p. 5). As in "The Autobiography of Rose" (besides *Four in America*), Stein is preoccupied with the problem of attributing an identity to a certain name, of assuming to be somebody else, and she articulates this question in a direct and simple way that children may understand. The preceding paragraph is almost identical to a passage from "The Autobiography of Rose"; thus, Stein uses parts of previous texts belonging to entirely different discourses—in this case one meant to be read by adults. But as long as the topic is the same, Stein does not differentiate between her audiences—be they adults or children.

As mentioned above, the topic of both children's book and "autobiography" (of Rose) is identity, and in both books a little girl is trying to find out who she is. Both explore the relationship between name, person, and identity. For Stein, it does not matter whether Rose writes "her" autobiography under Stein's name ("To Rose . . . Gertrude Stein") or whether Rose in *The World Is Round* goes around the round world, that is, in a circle, stating at the end "Rose is Rose" (p. 59). The ever-returning question about a person's identity refers to oneself[1]—in Stein's case, to herself: auto–bio–graphos.

Wondering about her identity makes Rose cry at the very beginning of the book; her worries stem from her doubts about her name. But Rose is also saddened by what she learns at school, namely that the world is round. She does not believe this because of the mountains she has seen: They are high and "they could stop anything" (p. 15). For Rose the mountains represent power that could even impede the continuity of a circle because she perceives roundness as something threatening. Remembering her own image with her mouth open and "round" in a mirror[2] when she was little, she is deeply troubled. The reference to a kind of "mirror stage" in the Lacanian sense of the word stresses the relationship between language and identity and may illustrate Stein's awareness of this connection.[3] As Lacan points out, this moment in a child's life is only realized retrospectively,[4] which is exactly what happens with Rose. She is a girl experiencing growing up, which means acquiring an identity through language.

As mentioned in Chapter 14 there are a few incidents in "The Autobiography of Rose" that appear to be threatening to the little girl, among them the reference to the little boy (p. 39). A little boy also appears in *The World Is Round*; his name is Willy and, in contrast to Rose, he is neither worried about his name nor does he assume any connection between name and identity:

My name is Willy I am not like Rose
I would be Willy whatever arose,
I would be Willy if Henry was my name
I would be Willy always Willy all the same. (p. 11)

The little girl Rose has a male counterpart who differs not only in sex but in other vital aspects of life. He says of himself that he "know[s] everything" and "do[es] everything" (p. 16), and we must interpret the following pun as an indirect comment: "Willy Will he" (pp. 16–17), as Willy and his willpower—Willy *will* do something—or simply as an instruction on how to pronounce his name. The pun on "willie" meaning penis in baby talk refers to the sexual dimension on this quest for female identity. A typical Steinian play with and in language enhances the different readings on the one hand, and creates pleasure and evokes laughter on the other. This double effect is very strongly present in this children's book with numerous puns, alliterations, rhymes, and the use of onomatopoeia, which are all particularly appreciated by children.[5] The line "I would be Willy whatever arose" also demonstrates this double meaning: Willy is always himself even if he were confronted with great difficulties, or he is himself even if he were together with Rose "a-Rose"). Thus, Willy, linguistically at least, is much more self-assured than Rose.

Nevertheless, Willy also undergoes a state of fear: The lion[6] he chooses for himself in the town of wild animals finally frightens him. Both he and Rose wonder why wild animals are wild. The inevitable answer is because the world is round—everything is determined because of this enormous law. Rose is depressed, but she can finally free herself from the lion and decides to climb a mountain in order to see the world. While Rose sets out on this journey, Willy disappears from the story until the end. Rose becomes the protagonist as in "The Autobiography of Rose." Her ascent reads like an autobiography of a person who undergoes various hardships and ordeals, and finally reaches her goal.

Rose decides to take a chair with her so she will be able to sit on top of the mountain, where she imagines finding a meadow; she and her blue[7] chair make this trip alone to the mountain. Stein describes the journey as if it were a quest for the Holy Grail. There are frightening creatures and rolling rocks, and Rose even finds the word "devil" written three times behind a waterfall. She is terrified by the mere word, although the narrator assures us that "of course there was no devil there there is no devil anywhere devil devil devil where" (p. 45). In spite of all these hardships, Rose does "not want Willy" (p. 43) and keeps on ascending. In the morning after the frightening night, "Rose Does Something" (this is the title of the chapter, p. 50). The enormous act is to carve her name around a tree with a pen-knife: "Rose is a Rose is a Rose is a Rose is a Rose until it went all the way round" (p. 50). The description of this carving illustrates the importance of naming (oneself); Rose is so entirely absorbed in this act of carving her name that she forgets her surroundings, her loneliness. Like Easter in Eudora Welty's *The Golden Apples*, who writes her (real) name, Esther, into the sand and says "I let myself name myself,"[8] Rose demonstrates strength, triumph, and self-assertion.

Rose's carving carries a further symbolic meaning: The tree with its phallic connotation is circumscribed by Rose with a circle. Indeed, her female identity is emphasized by "the curves of the Os and the Rs and Ss and Es in a Rose is a Rose is a Rose is a Rose" (p. 51). Significantly, the "O" is mentioned first, representing the female circle/cycle. Considering Rose's fear of roundness, we may say that Rose is proud of her name (and its "roundness"), but she is also afraid of her budding female sexuality. When she discovers another tree on which is carved "Rose and under Rose was Willy and under Willy was Billie [the lion]" (p. 51), "she feel[s] very funny" (p. 51) and wants to climb on. She finally reaches the green meadow immediately before reaching the top of the mountain.

Being so close to her goal triggers another crisis: Rose can no longer distinguish between green and blue, between one and two; it is as if she loses all balance and orientation.[9] But she overcomes this imbalance by strictly counting "one two one two" (p. 56). She does not let herself be distracted because she is bent on reaching the top of the mountain, and indeed, while still counting, she perceives a rainbow that leads her to the top. Her identity is not fragmented into blue or green, so to speak, but is whole in the sense that it is "one two one two one two" and so on. I have mentioned before that Stein's "I" is never one but two or more; this incident of counting up to two also hints at the necessary focus on one and "another," that is, two in order to remain whole.[10] Thus, Rose as a whole person reaches the summit, where she sits on her blue chair and begins to sing a song. Now the song, in contrast to the one at the beginning of the story, expresses self-confidence and reflects acceptance of her name, although at first Rose sings about her doubts concerning the referentiality of things and persons:

> Am I here or am I there,
> Is the chair a bed or is it a chair.
> Who is where.
> . . .
> I am Rose my eyes are blue
> I am Rose and who are you
> I am Rose and when I sing
> I am Rose like anything. (p. 59)

Having named herself again (on the tree), Rose can utter who she is in spite of the fact that the ever-recurring question "who is where" or actually "who is who?" (we must be susceptible to the pun of German "wer?") persists in Stein's writing—even in a children's book with a so-called happy ending. Nevertheless, Rose feels terribly frightened and lonesome on this chair on a mountain, and when she sees a light going round on another hill, she realizes that it comes from Willy. Willy's searchlight comforts Rose, although the light is revolving. Why Willy uses a searchlight in this scene is not explained. Considering the conventional (fairy tale) happy ending—namely that Rose and Willy get married (it turns out they are not cousins after all), "and they lived happily ever after and the world just went on being round" (p. 60)—I suggest that Willy is searching for Rose. Strangely enough, Rose calls him "Will" in this last section, expressing a certain incantatory intention: "Oh Will oh Will / A little boy upon a hill. / He will oh will. / Oh Will oh Will" (p. 61). Here Stein again implies a verbal pleasure that need not necessarily be connected with Rose's real desire.

The ending is disconcerting after Rose's emancipatory climb all by herself and without Willy's help; it seems as if Stein made concessions to a conciliatory conclusion for her children's book. Richard Bridgman even states that Rose and Willy's marriage at the end "betrays the book's fundamental mood," which is "dark and sad."[11] In spite of this structural happy ending, the narrator draws our attention to Rose's persisting sadness whenever she sings, in contrast to singing Willy who "get[s] more and more excited" (p. 62). Rose has accepted the world's roundness as it were, and has overcome a tremendous struggle of self-doubt, but the sadness about her identity remains. Her songs mainly trigger her gloomy state of mind, and one could draw a parallel between song and text, that is, writing, in that both require a form that is recognizable by an audience and is also received by such as one. Rose represents another "Mother of Us All," who explores her life in a never-ending circle by using language: voice and word (vote).

A comparison between *The World Is Round* and "The Autobiography of Rose" supports this conclusion because in both texts, Rose is described as a girl who challenges word, (her) name, and identity, and yet remains entirely dependent on language/writing. As the narrator in "The Autobiography of Rose" states with emphasis, Gertrude Stein, the writer, is Rose's friend and companion. Stein is eager to establish a close connection between the author and the narrative voice. As I have demonstrated earlier in my study, the borderline between text and life and between writing and author is very thin; Stein's texts are full of references to her own life and yet they constantly pose the questions Who is where? or Who are you? The crucial question Who am *I*? is never expressed explicitly, but it is implied in Stein's dialogic discourse that always addresses an(other) "you."

The dialogic principle as it appears in this children's book is closely intertwined with Rose, the little girl. The questions challenging identity are primarily expressed by Rose herself and not, for example, by Willy, her male companion. The female and male sex exemplarily represented here by Rose and Willy differ from each other because of the ways in which identity is attributed: Rose's is in process, searching and always calling into question the relation between name and person, whereas Willy's is a less complex, less challenging notion of self. Willy appears more as a supplement to the story ("autobiography") of Rose, and his character is not as fully developed. The categories "female" and "male" cannot be applied to Rose or Willy to describe their behavior, but the attributions "little girl"=Rose and "little boy"=Willy are made; this attribution with regard to the characters is therefore also germane to the ways their identities are constructed through the text. Gender as a category functions through the conventional pair "little girl"/"little boy," whereas the genre is determined by this very pair on the one hand, and is dissolved by the fact that the children's book must be read as another "autobiography of Rose" on the other hand. When we establish such an interrelation between gender and genre, it becomes evident that they determine each other in Stein's texts, but at the same time are annihilated through Stein's constant questioning of the notion of identity. Composing via rearranging means that concepts such as genre and gender are flexible and not definable in the end because they are changing positions all the time. What matters is that "composition is different" and this "difference is spreading."[12]

NOTES

1. Jean Marcet emphasizes this reference to oneself in an early essay on *The World Is Round*, stating that Stein's writing reflects a circular trajectory that moves from self to self. "Le cercle enchanté," in *Delta* 10, (May 1980): 17.

2. Stein uses the words "looking glass," which may be an allusion to Lewis Carroll's *Through the Looking-Glass*.

3. Interestingly enough, Lacan gave his lecture on "Le stade du miroir" in 1936, which was published in English in *The International Journal of Psychoanalysis*, vol. 18, part I (January 1937), under the title "The Looking-glass Phase." I do not know if Stein knew of this article.

4. See Kaja Silverman, *The Subject of Semiotics* (New York: Oxford University Press, 1983), p. 161.

5. When I read the book (in a German translation that retains many of these devices) to my nine-year-old son, his frequent laughter corroborated this point.

6. The pun "lion"/"lie on" implies a further sexual connotation with regard to Willy.

7. For a discussion of the color blue, see Bridgman, *Gertrude Stein in Pieces*, p. 303.

8. Eudora Welty, *The Golden Apples* (New York: Harcourt Brace Jovanovich, 1949), p. 133.

9. Bridgman speaks of a disintegration of Rose's identity; she cannot control her imagination anymore. *Gertrude Stein in Pieces*, p. 303.

10. For a slightly different reading of this passage, see Bridgman, p. 303, where he comments on the danger of multiplying. He states that through counting, Rose can retain "her ability to control imagination."

11. Ibid., p. 304.

12. Stein, *Tender Buttons*, in *Selected Writings of Gertrude Stein*, ed. Van Vechten, p. 461.

Appendix:
Stein's Manuscripts

Sitting in the Beineke Rare Book and Manuscript Library and studying Gertrude Stein's notebooks[1] I was deeply touched by their smallness. These tiny *cahiers* hold immense wisdom and give evidence of enormous creativity in many fields and yet their appearance seems to imply that they are full of coincidental remarks jotted down, practical information, travel notes, etc. In any case, these notebooks do not correspond to the expectations a reader might have of Gertrude Stein, namely of grandness and of extensiveness in both language and personality. Yet, reading the notebooks, one is confronted with a handwriting that does corroborate these expectations: long and large letters are strewn over the small pages; only a few lines cover a page, thus a wide realm is kept open, an empty space. One notebook, for example, has only five lines with seven squares between each line.[2]

Another idiosyncracy of Stein's compositional process is her writing in the notebooks from both ends—that is, there are often two different topics or works (sometimes with titles), one beginning from the front, the other from the back, but the back becomes the front when it is turned upside down. This reverse approach also shows that Stein was definitely working on more than one work at a time; the end of the section "Regular Regularly in Narrative" from *How to Write* is, for example, in the notebook of *Four Saints in Three Acts*.[3] Working on two or more different texts left traces in each text, that is, at least in these two texts. *Four Saints in Three Acts*, also written in 1927, is one of the better known operas, mainly because of its stage history and its music by Virgil Thomson. Its first performance in 1934 was a great success and provoked a lot of publicity.[4]

Comparing the two texts, *Four Saints in Three Acts* and "Regular Regularly in Narrative," a number of similarities can be detected, although the former is "An Opera to Be Sung"[5] and the other a meditation on narrative. But we know by now that this generic label is not at all reliable, if not deliberately confusing to the reader or spectator. Apart from this generic mistrust, here the "blurring of genres" is illuminating because the piece on narrative comments on the opera and vice versa. The beginning of *Four Saints in Three Acts* refers to a certain narrative that "prepare[s] for saints" (p. 440). Indeed, it seems as if this "regular narrative" is about the plan to write an opera: "A narrative to plan an opera. / Four saints in three acts" (p. 443), and yet this comment belongs to the opera. In "Regular Regularly in Narrative," a plan for an opera is also mentioned: "Preparing for opera."[6] Other references to Stein's work on an opera about Saint Teresa are combined with her concern about exploring the possibilities of a narrative. The following example illustrates the combination of personal reminiscences, theoretical comments on narrative, and practical matters of how to tackle an opera about Saint Teresa of Avila.

An [*sic*] a narrative of irregularity.
A narrative of relatively [*sic*].
She wants to talk about the Jesuits about whose adventures it is very interesting to note repeatedly.
If it has been asked not to stay to leave not to stay to leave not to stay if it has been asked not to stay relatively to leave not to stay if it has been asked to leave relatively not to stay to leave not to stay. (p. 242)

The personal memory probably refers to Alice B. Toklas, who wanted to stay on when she and Stein visited Avila in 1912.[7] The illogical vocabulary of the discussion between the two women, "not to stay or to leave," gradually takes over the crucial word from ideas about narrative, "a narrative of *relatively*." The reference to the Jesuits hints at Saint Ignatius of Loyola, who is a protagonist in the opera. In *Four Saints in Three Acts*, Stein also provides several explanations as to why she chose this character. In the opera itself, the search for and the choice of certain characters are discussed.[8] The writer describes the writing process like a plot and creates a contemporaneity of the process and the result, that is, the text—something one would expect to find in a piece such as *How to Write* but not in a play or an opera.

Stein's habit of writing into these French notebooks and usually using one for more than one particular work represents in various ways her creative activity as an artist: it shows that Stein was always writing and, thus, writing on diverse topics. The confluence, or blurring, of these texts in the outer form of these notebooks created new texts, but their traits also appeared in other, later texts, or were inserted in earlier texts. Composing texts for Stein also meant listening to or reading what it was she had written before, and at any moment a new text could be created. A generic plan would have been an obstacle to this process. Nevertheless, by choosing labels, Stein could evoke expectations and yet proceed as her creative mind for composition demanded. Creating while writing equally implied living her life in dialogue with another "you," in her case with Alice B. Toklas, a different person of the same sex; thus, gender infused her writing because Stein created new ways of looking and writing: looking at the heterosexual patterns surrounding her and writing herself out of patriarchy.

The manuscripts of *The Making of Americans* demonstrate in detail how Stein's investigation of gender traits goes hand in hand with the creative process of writing this "history of a family's progress." In one of the notebooks for the "Studies for *The Making of Americans*," Toklas is described in the following words: "Alice is of the St. Therese type," or with reference to George Elliot [*sic*] she is "St. Therese's type in fact very close to her. Alice's resemblance to George Elliot interesting in this connection."[9] We know that in *The Making of Americans*, Stein tries to set up categories to describe different people; her comparison of Toklas to George Eliot and St. Teresa is revealing in that it reflects Stein's reliance on women whose biographies mirror independence, autonomy, and nontraditional gender roles.[10] The following reference to another woman novelist is a further link in this chain of prominent female characters: "George Sand undoubtedly is of George Elliot's, Alice's family, that's easy."[11]

Although Stein does not make direct use of these comparisons in *The Making of Americans*, we know how crucial gender traits are for her classifications. The manuscripts certainly give more evidence of the ways gender is constructed through Stein's experience with people and texts (mainly by women authors). Looking at different people and comparing them to each other and to persons she knew through their works, Stein established categories that reflect the close interaction between life and text. A remark about her brother's philosophical orientation in contrast to her own in the same notebook is illuminating in this respect; Stein emphasizes her belief in art, which, according to her, is closer to reality than Leo Stein's pragmatism[12]:

When Leo said that all classification is teleological I knew I was not a pragmatist I do not believe that. I believe in reality as Cezanne [*sic*] or Caliban believe in it. I believe in repetition. Yes. Always and always.[13]

For Stein, Cézanne is crucial because in his paintings each piece of his composition was equally important, and each detail existed in its own right. Her concept of repetition also implies that there is no such thing as repetition because as soon as you repeat something, the thing repeated is no longer the same; thus, "everything is not the same," and therefore everything is crucial in a composition. This very composition is nothing separate from reality according to Stein; therefore, she mentions Cézanne and Caliban together, the former representing art, the latter reality, that is, nature. A different reading of Stein's reference to Cézanne and Caliban is that both believe in reality, except that the artist creates a new composition of it.

Writing into her *cahiers* and composing reality anew, Stein did not want to adhere to literary categories such as genre; instead, her compositions engendered new forms.

NOTES

1. Stein took notes almost anywhere and any time, even when sitting in her car. The notebooks she mainly used are French schoolchildren's *cahiers*—most of which have a cover with a picture. Sometimes these illustrations served to inspire her. See also Bridgman, *Gertrude Stein in Pieces*, p. 22.

2. Notebook, *Arthur A Grammarian* (1928), orig. ms. 368.

3. Notebook, "Regular Regularly in Narrative" (1927), orig. ms. 346. On Notebook V of this manuscript it says in Stein's handwriting that the continuation can be found in vol. of *Four Saints in Three Acts*.

4. See Mellow, *Charmed Circle: Gertrude Stein & Company* (New York: Praeger, 1974), pp. 368–70; Bridgman, *Gertrude Stein in Pieces*, p. 176; or Diana Souhami, *Gertrude and Alice* (London: Pandora, 1991), pp. 198–201.

5. Stein, *Four Saints in Three Acts* in *Last Operas and Plays*, p. 440.

6. Stein, "Regular Regularly in Narrative," in *How to Write*, p. 250. Further references in the text refer to this edition.

7. See Mellow, *Charmed Circle*, p. 305.

8. Jane Palatini Bowers also comments on this topic of Stein's plans in *Four Saints in Three Acts*, in *They Watch Me as They Watch This*, pp. 39–40, 50–52.

9. "Studies for *The Making of Americans*," Box I, notebook D.

10. For an illuminating reading of the life and works of St. Teresa, see Alison Weber, *Teresa of Avila and the Rhetoric of Femininity* (Princeton, NJ: Princeton University Press, 1990). Weber also mentions that Teresa was, like Stein, of Jewish ancestry (p. 8). In connection with Stein's fascination with St. Teresa on the one hand, and with her favorite author George Eliot on the other, one must mention the important symbolic function the figure and myth of St. Teresa plays in George Eliot's prelude to her novel *Middlemarch*. As we know from Stein's manuscripts, Stein was deeply impressed by Eliot's novels, especially by *The Mill on the Floss*. In the "Radcliffe Manuscripts" we find a story called "In the Red Deeps," following George Eliot. See "The Radcliffe Manuscripts," in Rosalind S. Miller, *Gertrude Stein: Form and Intelligibility* (New York: Exposition Press, 1949), pp. 108–10.

11. "Studies for *The Making of Americans*," box 1, notebook D.

12. See, for example, John Malcolm Brinnin, *The Third Rose: Gertrude Stein and Her World* (Boston: Little, Brown, 1959), pp. 43–55.

13. "Studies for *The Making of Americans*," box 1, notebook D.

Bibliography

BOOKS BY STEIN

The Autobiography of Alice B. Toklas. New York: Random House, 1961.

Bee Time Vine and Other Pieces [1913–1927]. Yale Edition of the Unpublished Writings of Gertrude Stein. New Haven, CT: Yale University Press, 1953.

Blood on the Dining-Room Floor. Ed. John Herbert Gill. Berkeley, CA: Creative Arts Book Company, 1982.

Everybody's Autobiography. New York: Random House, 1937.

Fernhurst, Q.E.D., and Other Early Writings. London: Peter Owen, 1972.

Four in America. New Haven, CT: Yale University Press, 1947.

The Geographical History of America or The Relation of Human Nature to the Human Mind. New York: Random House, 1936.

Geography and Plays. 1922. Reprint, New York: Haskell House, 1967.

How to Write. New York: Dover Publications, 1975.

How Writing Is Written: Volume II of the Previously Uncollected Writings by Gertrude Stein. Ed. Robert Bartlett Haas. Los Angeles: Black Sparrow Press, 1974.

Ida A Novel. New York: Random House, 1968.

Last Operas and Plays. Ed. Carl Van Vechten. New York: Rinehart, 1949.

Lectures in America. Boston: Beacon Press, 1985.

The Making of Americans: Being a History of a Family's Progress. New York: Something Else Press, 1966.

Matisse, Picasso and Gertrude Stein with Two Shorter Stories. Barton, VT: Something Else Press, 1972.

Narration. Four Lectures by Gertrude Stein. Chicago: University of Chicago Press, 1935.

Operas and Plays. 1932. Reprint, Barrytown, NY: Station Hill Press, 1987. Foreword by James R. Mellow.

Painted Lace and Other Pieces [1914–1937]. Yale Edition of the Unpublished Writings of Gertrude Stein. New Haven, CT: Yale University Press, 1955. Reprint, New York: Books for Libraries Press, 1969.

Paris France. New York: Liveright, 1970.

Picasso. New York: Dover Publications, 1984.

Reflection on the Atomic Bomb: *Vol. I of the Previously Uncollected Writings of Gertrude Stein*. Ed. Robert Bartlett Haas. Los Angeles: Black Sparrow Press, 1975.

Selected Writings of Gertrude Stein. Ed. Carl Van Vechten. New York: Random House, 1962.

Stanzas in Meditation and Other Poems [1929–1933]. Yale Edition of the Unpublished Writings of Gertrude Stein. New Haven, CT: Yale University Press, 1956.

A Stein Reader. Ed. Ulla E. Dydo. Evanston, IL: Northwestern University Press, 1993.

"A Transatlantic Interview 1946." In *Gertrude Stein: A Primer for the Gradual Understanding of Gertrude Stein*. Ed. Robert Bartlett Haas. Los Angeles: Black Sparrow, 1971, pp. 15–35.

Two: Gertrude Stein and Her Brother and Other Early Portraits [1908–12]. Yale Edition of the Unpublished Writings of Gertrude Stein. New Haven, CT: Yale University Press, 1951.

Useful Knowledge. Foreword by Edward Burns. Introduction by Keith Waldrop. Barrytown, NY: Station Hill Press, 1988.

Wars I Have Seen. New York: Random House, 1945.

What Are Masterpieces and Why Are There So Few of Them. Los Angeles: The Conference Press, 1940.

The World Is Round. London: William Clowes and Sons, 1939.

The Yale Gertrude Stein. Ed. Richard Kostelanetz. New Haven, CT: Yale University Press, 1980.

WORKS CITED

Abel, Elizabeth. Ed. *Writing and Sexual Difference*. Chicago: University of Chicago Press, 1982.

Adams, Timothy Dow. "Life Writing and Light Writing: Autobiography and Photography." *Modern Fiction Studies* 40, no. 3 (Fall 1994): 459–92.

Alkon, Paul K. "Visual Rhetoric in *The Autobiography of Alice B. Toklas*." *Critical Inquiry* 1, no. 4 (June 1975): 849–81.

Antin, David. "Some Questions about Modernism." An Excerpt. In *Gertrude Stein Advanced: An Anthology of Criticism*. Ed. Richard Kostelanetz. Jefferson, NC: McFarland, 1990, pp. 208–12.

Ashbery, John. "The Impossible." In *Critical Essays on Gertrude Stein*. Ed. Michael Hoffman. Boston: G. K. Hall, 1986, pp. 104–7.

Barry, Kathleen. *Susan B. Anthony: A Biography of a Singular Feminist*. New York: New York University Press, 1988.

Barzun, Jacques. "Detection and Literary Art." In *Detective Fiction: A Collection of Critical Essays*. Ed. Robin W. Winks. Englewood Cliffs, NJ: Prentice-Hall, 1980, pp. 144–53.

Bennett, Tony. Ed. *Popular Fiction: Technology, Ideology, Production, Reading*. London: Routledge, 1990.

Benstock, Shari. "Beyond the Reaches of Feminist Criticism: A Letter from Paris." In *Feminist Issues in Literary Scholarship*. Ed. Shari Benstock. Bloomington: Indiana University Press, 1987, pp. 7–29.

———. "From Letters to Literature: La Carte Postale in the Epistolary Genre." *Genre* 18, no. 3 (Fall 1985): 257–95.

————. *Textualizing the Feminine: On the Limits of Genre*. Norman: University of Oklahoma Press, 1991.

————. *Women of the Left Bank: Paris 1900–1940*. Austin: University of Texas Press, 1986.

Berry, Ellen E. *Curved Thought and Textual Wandering: Gertrude Stein's Postmodernism*. Ann Arbor: University of Michigan Press, 1992.

Blake, Nancy. Ed. *Delta* 10 (May 1980).

Blankley, Elyse. "Beyond the 'Talent of Knowing': Gertrude Stein and the New Woman." In *Critical Essays on Gertrude Stein*. Ed. Michael J. Hoffman. Boston: G. K. Hall, 1986, pp. 196–209.

Bloom, Harold. Ed. *Gertrude Stein*. New York: Chelsea House, 1986.

Bowers, Jane Palatini. *"They Watch Me as They Watch This": Gertrude Stein's Metadrama*. Philadelphia: University of Pennsylvania Press, 1991.

Breslin, James E. "Gertrude Stein and the Problems of Autobiography." *Georgia Review* 33, no. 4 (Winter 1979): 901–13.

Bridgman, Richard. *Gertrude Stein in Pieces*. New York: Oxford University Press, 1970.

Brinnin, John Malcolm. *The Third Rose*. Boston: Little, Brown, 1959.

Brodzki, Bella, and Celeste Schenck. Eds. *Life/Lines: Theorizing Women's Autobiography*. Ithaca, NY: Cornell University Press, 1988.

Burke, Carolyn. "Gertrude Stein, the Cone Sisters, and the Puzzle of Female Friendship." *Critical Inquiry* 8, no. 3 (Spring 1982): 543–64.

Bush, Clive. "Towards the Outside: The Quest for Discontinuity in Gertrude Stein's *The Making of Americans: Being a History of a Family's Progress*." *Twentieth Century Literature* 24 (Spring 1978): 27–56.

Butler, Judith. *Bodies That Matter: On the Discursive Limits of "Sex."* New York: Routledge, 1993.

————. *Gender Trouble: Feminism and the Subversion of Identity*. New York and London: Routledge, 1990.

Cagidemetrio, Alide, Barbara Lanati, and Bianca Tarozzi. *La Signora Plusvalore: Gertrude Stein*. Bologna: Pitagora Editrice, 1979.

Caramello, Charles. "Reading Gertrude Stein Reading Henry James, or Eros Is Eros Is Eros Is Eros." *Henry James Review* 6, no. 3 (Spring 1985): 182–203.

Carr, Helen. Ed. *From My Guy to Sci-Fi: Genre and Women's Writing in the Postmodern World*. London: Pandora, 1989.

Chessman, Harriet. *The Public Is Invited to Dance: Representation, the Body, and Dialogue in Gertrude Stein*. Stanford, CA: Stanford University Press, 1989.

Cixous, Hélène. "The Laugh of the Medusa." In *New French Feminisms*. Ed. Elaine Marks and Isabelle de Courtivron. New York: Schocken Books, 1981, pp. 245–64.

Cohen, Ralph. "Do Postmodern Genres Exist?" In *Postmodern Genres*. Ed. Marjorie Perloff. Norman: University of Oklahoma Press, 1989, pp. 11–27.

Copeland, Carolyn Faunce. *Language & Time & Gertrude Stein*. Iowa City: University of Iowa Press, 1975.

Dachy, Marc. Ed. *Gertrude Stein*. Cahiers du Grif 21–22 (September 1978).

Darras, Jacques. Ed. *Gertrude Stein, Encore. in'Hui* 0 (April 1983).

Davy, Kate. "Richard Foreman's Ontological-Hysteric Theatre: The Influence of Gertrude Stein." *Twentieth Century Literature* 24 (Spring 1978): 108–26.

DeKoven, Marianne. *A Different Language: Gertrude Stein's Experimental Writing*. Madison: University of Wisconsin Press, 1983.

————. "Gertrude Stein's Landscape Writing." *Women's Studies* 9 (1982): 221–39.

Derrida, Jacques. "The Law of Genre." *Critical Inquiry* 7, no. 1 (Autumn 1980): 55–81.

Doane, Janice Louise. *Silence and Narrative: The Early Novels of Gertrude Stein*. Westport, CT: Greenwood Press, 1986.

Dubnick, Randa. *The Structure of Obscurity: Gertrude Stein, Language, and Cubism*. Urbana: University of Illinois Press, 1984.

Dubrow, Heather. *Genre*. London: Methuen, 1982.

Dydo, Ulla E. "Gertrude Stein: Composition as Meditation." In *Gertrude Stein and the Making of Literature*. Ed. Shirley Neuman and Ira B. Nadel. London: Macmillan, 1988, pp. 42–60.

————. "Must Horses Drink; or, 'Any Language Is Funny If You Don't Understand It.'" *Tulsa Studies in Women's Literature* 4 (1985): 272–80.

————. "*Stanzas in Meditation*: The Other Autobiography." *Chicago Review* 35, no. 2 (Winter 1985): 4–20.

Ecker, Gisela. "Gertrude Stein, Hilda Doolittle (H.D.) und Djuna Barnes: Drei Amerikanerinnen in Europa." In *Weiblichkeit und Avantgarde*. Ed. Inge Stephan and Sigrid Weigel. Hamburg: Argument-Verlag, 1987, pp. 40–66.

Elam, Keir. *The Semiotics of Theatre and Drama*. London: Methuen, 1980.

Engelbrecht, Penelope J. "'Lifting Belly Is a Language': The Postmodern Lesbian Subject." *Feminist Studies* 16, no. 1 (Spring 1990): 85–114.

Felski, Rita. *Beyond Feminist Aesthetics: Feminist Literature and Social Change*. Cambridge, MA: Harvard University Press, 1989.

Fifer, Elizabeth. "'In Conversation': Gertrude Stein's Speaker, Message, and Receiver in *Painted Lace and Other Pieces [1914–1937]*." *Modern Fiction Studies* 34, no. 3 (Autumn 1988): 465–80.

————. "Is Flesh Advisable? The Interior Theater of Gertrude Stein." *Signs* 4 (Spring 1979): 472–83.

————. *Rescued Readings: A Reconstruction of Gertrude Stein's Difficult Texts*. Detroit: Wayne State University Press, 1992.

Fowler, Alastair. *Kinds of Literature: An Introduction to the Theory of Genres and Modes*. Oxford: Oxford University Press, 1982.

Fredman, Stephen. *Poet's Prose: The Crisis in American Verse*. Cambridge: Cambridge University Press, 1983.

Gass, William H. "Gertrude Stein and the Geography of the Sentence." In *The World Within the World*. Boston: David R. Godine, 1979, pp. 63–123.

Geertz, Clifford. "Blurred Genres: The Refiguration of Social Thought." *The American Scholar* 49 (Spring 1980): 165–79.

Gerhart, Mary. *Genre Choices, Gender Questions*. Norman: University of Oklahoma Press, 1992.

Gibbs, Anna. "Hélène Cixous and Gertrude Stein: New Directions in Feminist Criticism." *Meanjin* 38, no. 3 (September 1979): 281–93.

Hadas, Pamela. "Spreading the Difference: One Way to Read Gertrude Stein's *Tender Buttons*." *Twentieth Century Literature* 24 (Spring 1978): 57–75.

Hoffman, Michael J. Ed. *Critical Essays on Gertrude Stein*. Boston: G. K. Hall, 1986.

Hoffmann, Monika. *Gertrude Steins Autobiographien: The Autobiography of Alice B. Toklas und Everybody's Autobiography*. Frankfurt am Main: Peter Lang, 1992.

Hubert, Renée Riese. "Gertrude Stein, Cubism, and the Postmodern Book." In *Postmodern Genres*. Ed. Marjorie Perloff. Norman: University of Oklahoma Press, 1989, pp. 96–125.

Hunt, Peter. *Criticism, Theory, and Children's Literature*. Oxford: Basil Blackwell, 1991.

Katz, Leon. "Weininger and *The Making of Americans.*" *Twentieth Century Literature* 24 (Spring 1978): 8–26.

Kauffman, Linda. *Discourses of Desire: Gender, Genre, and Epistolary Fictions.* Ithaca, NY: Cornell University Press, 1986.

Kellner, Bruce. Ed. *A Gertrude Stein Companion: Content with the Example.* New York: Greenwood Press, 1988.

Kostelanetz, Richard. Ed. *Gertrude Stein Advanced: An Anthology of Criticism.* Jefferson, NC: McFarland, 1990.

Martin, Robert K. "*The Mother of Us All* and American History." In *Gertrude Stein and the Making of Literature.* Ed. Shirley Neuman and Ira B. Nadel. London: Macmillan, 1988, pp. 210–22.

Mellow, James R. *Charmed Circle: Gertrude Stein and Company.* New York: Praeger, 1974.

Miller, Nancy K. "Changing the Subject: Authorship, Writing, and the Reader." In *Feminist Studies/Cultural Studies.* Ed. Teresa de Lauretis. Bloomington: Indiana University Press, 1986, pp. 102–20.

———. *Getting Personal: Feminist Occasions and Other Autobiographical Acts.* New York: Routledge, 1991.

Miller, Rosalind S. *Gertrude Stein: Form and Intelligibility.* New York: Exposition Press, 1949.

Minh-ha, Trinh T. *When the Moon Waxes Red: Representation Gender and Cultural Politics.* New York: Routledge, 1991.

Moi, Toril. Ed. *The Kristeva Reader.* New York: Columbia University Press, 1986.

Moretti, Franco. "Clues." In *Popular Fiction: Technology, Ideology, Production, Reading.* Ed. Tony Bennett. London: Routledge, 1990, pp. 238–51.

Neuman, Shirley, and Ira B. Nadel. Eds. *Gertrude Stein and the Making of Literature.* London: Macmillan, 1988.

Nichol, bp. "When the Time Came." In *Gertrude Stein and the Making of Literature.* Ed. Shirley Neuman, and Ira B. Nadel. London: Macmillan, 1988, pp. 194–209.

Pasquier, Marie-Claire. "Gertrude Stein: un théâtre 'postmoderne'?" *Delta.* 10 (May 1980): 43–58.

Perloff, Marjorie. "'A Fine New Kind of Realism': Six Stein Styles in Search of a Reader." In *Poetic License: Essays on Modernist and Postmodernist Lyric.* Ed. Marjorie Perloff. Evanston, IL: Northwestern University Press, 1990, 145–59.

———. Ed. *Postmodern Genres.* Norman: University of Oklahoma Press, 1989.

Pladott, Dinnah. "Gertrude Stein: Exile, Feminism, Avant-Garde in the American Theater." In *Modern American Drama: The Female Canon.* Ed. June Schlueter. Rutherford, NJ: Fairleigh Dickinson University Press, 1990.

Retallack, Joan. "Post-Scriptum—High-Modern." In *Postmodern Genres.* Ed. Marjorie Perloff. Norman: University of Oklahoma Press, 1989, pp. 248–74.

Rose, Jacqueline. *Sexuality in the Field of Vision.* London: Verso, 1986.

Rosmarin, Adena. *The Power of Genre.* Minneapolis: University of Minnesota Press, 1985.

Ruddick, Lisa. *Reading Gertrude Stein: Body, Text, Gnosis.* Ithaca, NY: Cornell University Press, 1990.

———. "A Rosy Charm: Gertrude Stein and the Repressed Feminine." In *Critical Essays on Gertrude Stein.* Ed. Michael Hoffman. Boston: G. K. Hall, 1986, pp. 225–40.

Ryan, Betsy Alayne. *Gertrude Stein's Theatre of the Absolute.* Ann Arbor, MI: U.M.I. Research Press, 1980.

Schlaeger, Jürgen. *Grenzen der Moderne: Gertrude Steins Prosa.* Konstanz: Universitätsverlag Konstanz, 1978.

Schmitz, Neil. "The Difference of Her Likeness." In *Gertrude Stein and the Making of Literature.* Ed. Shirley Neuman, and Ira B. Nadel. London: Macmillan, 1988, pp. 124–49.

———. *Of Huck and Alice: Humorous Writing in American Literature.* Minneapolis: University of Minnesota Press, 1983.

———. "Portrait, Patriarchy, Mythos: The Revenge of Gertrude Stein." *Salmagundi* 40 (Winter 1978): 69–91.

Secor, Cynthia. "*Ida,* A Great American Novel." *Twentieth Century Literature* 24 (Spring 1978): 96–107.

———. "The Question of Gertrude Stein." In *American Novelists Revisited: Essays in Feminist Criticism.* Ed. Fritz Fleischmann et al. Boston: G. K. Hall, 1982, pp. 299–310.

Silverman, Kaja. *The Subject of Semiotics.* New York: Oxford University Press, 1983.

Sitney, P. Adams. *Modernist Montage: The Obscurity of Vision in Cinema and Literature.* New York: Columbia University Press, 1990.

Smith, Sidonie. *A Poetics of Women's Autobiography: Marginality and the Fictions of Self-Representations.* Bloomington: Indiana University Press, 1987.

———. "Self, Subject, and Resistance: Marginalities and Twentieth-Century Autobiographical Practice." *Tulsa Studies in Women's Literature* 9, no. 1 (Spring 1990): 11–24.

Souhami, Diana. *Gertrude and Alice.* London: Pandora, 1991.

Sprigge, Elizabeth. *Gertrude Stein: Her Life and Work.* New York: Harper and Brothers, 1957.

Steiner, Wendy. *Exact Resemblance to Exact Resemblance: The Literary Portraiture of Gertrude Stein.* New Haven, CT: Yale University Press, 1978.

Stewart, Allegra. *Gertrude Stein and the Present.* Cambridge, MA: Harvard University Press, 1967.

Stimpson, Catharine R. "Gertrice/Altrude: Stein, Toklas, and the Paradox of the Happy Marriage." In *Mothering the Mind: Twelve Studies of Writers and Their Silent Partners.* Ed. Ruth Perry and Martine Watson Brownley. New York: Holmes and Meier, 1984, pp. 122–39.

———. "Gertrude Stein and the Lesbian Lie." In *American Women's Autobiography: Fea(s)ts of Memory.* Ed. Margo Cully. Madison: University of Wisconsin Press, 1992, pp. 152–66.

———. "Gertrude Stein and the Transposition of Gender." In *The Poetics of Gender.* Ed. Nancy K. Miller. New York: Columbia University Press, 1986, pp. 1–18.

———. "The Mind, the Body, and Gertrude Stein." *Critical Inquiry* 3, no. 3 (Spring 1977): 489–506.

Suleiman, Susan. *Subversive Intent: Gender, Politics, and the Avant-Garde.* Cambridge, MA: Harvard University Press, 1990.

Sutherland, Donald. *Gertrude Stein: A Biography of Her Work.* New Haven, CT: Yale University Press, 1951.

Tobin, Patricia. *Time and the Novel: The Genealogical Imperative.* Princeton, NJ: Princeton University Press, 1978.

Todorov, Tzvetan. *Genres in Discourse.* Trans. Catherine Porter. Cambridge: Cambridge University Press, 1990.

Walker, Jayne L. *The Making of a Modernist: Gertrude Stein from Three Lives to Tender Buttons.* Amherst: University of Massachusetts Press, 1984.

Weininger, Otto. *Sex and Character*. London: Heinemann, 1906.

White, Ray Lewis. Ed. *Sherwood Anderson/Gertrude Stein: Correspondence and Personal Essays*. Chapel Hill: University of North Carolina Press, 1972.

Wilcox, Wendell. "A Note on Stein and Abstraction." In *Gertrude Stein Advanced: An Anthology of Criticism*. Ed. Richard Kostelanetz. Jefferson, NC: McFarland, 1990, pp. 105–7.

Winston, Elizabeth. "Making History in *The Mother of Us All*." *Mosaic: Journal for the Interdisciplinary Study of Literature* 20, no. 4 (Fall 1987): 117–29.

Index

About the Author

FRANZISKA GYGAX is Lecturer in English at the University of Basel, where she teaches courses in American literature. Her previous books include *Serious Daring from Within: Female Narrative Strategies in Eudora Welty's Novels* (Greenwood, 1990).

ISBN 0-313-30755-5

EAN

9 780313 307553

90000>

HARDCOVER BAR CODE